# Swimming Through Adversity
## *Surviving a Lung Transplant*

Gavin Maitland

First published by Dog Ear Publishing
4011 Vincennes Road
Indianapolis, IN 46268
www.dogearpublishing.net

dog ear
PUBLISHING

ISBN: 978-145756-372-0

This book is printed on acid free paper.
Printed in the United States of America

To Julie, Zander & Riley

and

Noah Burton

Gavin Maitland is donating the proceeds from the sale of this book to organizations supporting lung transplant research, and organ, eye & tissue donation awareness.

*"Sweet are the uses of adversity"*
- Duke Senior, ***As You Like It***,
Act II, Scene I,
William Shakespeare

## Author's Disclaimer & Suggestions

I have no medical credentials or expertise whatsoever. Scenarios in this book are depictions of actual experiences, my interpretations of individual interviews, and a bunch of subjective observations. They may not be representative of what anyone else may experience. None of my statements have been evaluated by the Food & Drug Administration, and are not intended to diagnose, treat, cure, or prevent any disease. Consult your physician before beginning any exercise program. Whenever you feel like it, close your eyes, take a deep breath, and count to ten. And don't forget to thank your lucky stars that, whatever else happens today, you can breathe.

Gavin Maitland
Boulder, Colorado
March 14th, 2018

# CONTENTS

# CHAPTER ONE: WARM-UP

You don't come across lung transplants every day. Worldwide, just over four thousand are performed every year, half of which are in the United States. Lung transplants make up only about three percent of all organ transplant operations.

It is a treatment of last resort. No one would elect to undergo a lung transplant who didn't have to. It is usually the only option left for people suffering from end-stage lung diseases such as cystic fibrosis (a genetic condition that clogs the lungs with mucus) or COPD (chronic obstructive pulmonary disease) or pulmonary hypertension or idiopathic pulmonary fibrosis (an irreversible scarring of the lungs). The last one - a type of pulmonary fibrosis - dragged me into the world of lung transplant.

An organ transplant can be a cataclysmic event for an individual and his or her family. Survival can depend on a mercurial mix of unconnected factors: where you live (in Spain, the transplant rate is forty-six per million of population, in the United States it is thirty-two, in Germany it is ten), how old you are, how quickly your doctor can navigate the medical obstacle course of specialists at the right hospital and, of course, whether an organ becomes available at the time you need it and whether your body's immune system can be convinced to allow the organ to live. The process can last years and be a source of excruciating anxiety and distress to the whole family and beyond.

But, if it works, the results can be spectacular. This is the story of my lung transplant, as well as the three core elements of success: scientific genius, physical exercise, and a strong support system. It is also a tale of adventure, family, and inspiration. Beyond survival, I want to share how sometimes you can live life despite adversity. And, in some cases, because of adversity.

The decline of my lungs began with a persistent, dry cough when I was about thirty-five. At first, I waved it away as an irritant, but it would not leave. One doctor thought it was probably asthma. Another thought it was probably allergies. For years, I was dissatisfied with the lack of a diagnosis.

My tolerance for physical exercise lessened for the first time in my life; my breathing was laboured, and I became thinner and sicker. Still no one could tell me definitively what was wrong. Six years after the cough began, my wife frantically drove me to the hospital when I could not breathe. I read the anxiety on the faces of the hospital pulmonologists. The chest x-rays were a mass of white, my oxygen saturation level was below eighty-five percent (normal is above ninety-five percent) and I could barely stand.

Over the next few weeks, the bad news came thick and fast. I only had six months to live. My only chance of survival was a lung transplant. My chances of getting an organ were low. And then, after weeks of consultation, testing, appointments, and procedures, a transplant physician telephoned my wife and perfunctorily told her that they did not think I would survive the transplant operation, so they did not want me as patient any longer.

In the ensuing frenetic months, my wife contacted many transplant centers across the country, and tenaciously followed-up. Amidst an avalanche of rejections, one hospital eventually responded positively. Yes, we might be able to help, they said; come on over.

We hurriedly arranged the thousand-mile one-way plane ride, and before long, I was on a lung transplant waiting list. A whirlwind of events followed: the tragic death of a young man, the heart-wrenching decision by his family to donate his organs and the roller-coaster ride of logistics, twenty-first century medical brilliance, raw emotion, and an arduous recovery.

Prior to the operation, I could only breathe in short, shallow gasps. When I awoke from the anesthetic, I inhaled the deepest, longest, and most beautiful breath that I could ever imagine. Despite the searing pain in my torso, I felt like standing up on the bed and cheering.

People often refer to lung transplant as a "second wind," but medical experts emphasize that transplant is not a cure, simply the exchange of one acute condition for another. Pre-transplant, it means severe respiratory distress, exhaustion, weight-loss, and the constant feeling that you are about to suffocate in your own mucus. Post-transplant, it means organ and bone damage from the daily medications, as well as managing frequent infections and potential organ rejection from a weakened immune system. But it does mean breath. And it does mean life.

I often think about Winston Churchill's quip as a war correspondent. "Nothing in life is so exhilarating as to be shot at without result," he said. That accurately describes me. Having been shot at, surviving certainly feels exhilarating

Britain's National Health Service notes, "The outlook for people who've had a lung transplant has improved in recent years and it's expected to continue improving." What do they mean by "improving"? The British Transplantation Society estimates that around "nine out of ten people" survive the transplant operation itself, with "most of these surviving for at least a year after having the operation. About five out of ten people will survive for at least five years, with many people living for at least ten years."

Hmm. Five years? Ten years?

A few months after my transplant, I was talking to an inquisitive woman at a social event. She was curious about how long I'd live after the lung transplant. I was still absorbing the multitude of information I'd received, and I replied that the average survival time was five years.

"Five years?" she said in surprise. "Hardly seems worth it."

Although her breathtakingly vacuous comment abruptly severed the conversation, it did serve a purpose. Even if I had known for certain that I would drop dead at five years - or one year or one month - I would still have gone ahead with the operation (Incidentally, I spent my fifth transplant anniversary escaping from Alcatraz, but that's another story). The preciousness of a few extra weeks, days, hours, minutes or seconds of life is incontrovertible and immeasurable.

Any life-threatening illness is a life-changing experience. Winston Churchill, no stranger to adversity, also said, "A pessimist sees the difficulty in every opportunity; an optimist sees the opportunity in every difficulty." I like to think that I am an optimist who sees transplant as an opportunity to get closer to his family and friends and inspire others in his "difficulty."

To this end, I have rekindled my adolescent passion for swimming and physical exercise into outlandish aquatic adventures. I relish the planning, preparation, and participation in an epic physical challenge that provides an unparalleled sense of satisfaction and accomplishment.

The genesis of this book was the Alcatraz swim in 2013 where I swam with my children from Alcatraz Island to the shore. My initial objective for that swim was to demonstrate to myself that I could accomplish such a feat with my transplanted lungs. I wanted to prove to myself that I could beat the ominous post-lung transplant survival statistic of "fifty percent at five years" which was the sword of Damocles hanging over my head. The swim was symbolic of "escaping" from the mindset that my activities were restricted - even imprisoned - by my lung disease. I felt I had been set free to do whatever I wanted to do.

As well as achieving that goal, the open-water swim provided a unique opportunity to share a real-life adventure with my wife, Julie, and my inspiring children, son Zander (then thirteen) and daughter Riley (then eleven). Our achievement – especially at their young ages and the fact that they wanted to do it with their Dad – is the stuff of family folklore and memories. Julie's unflagging and enthusiastic support is always the backbone that enables us to undertake these adventures. Without the perspective of a lung transplant, I don't know if I would have been adventurous to this extent.

On the flight home after the Alcatraz swim, I began to subconsciously formulate the activities of the swim into a written piece. I still smile to myself when I recall Zander and Riley's electrified reaction to the initial plunge into the cold water.

The first expedition swim was followed by crossings of Boston harbor, bridge-to-bridge in San Francisco, and New York harbor, with some fourteeners, and other adventures thrown in. The mother of my donor, Pam Burton, graciously agreed for her son Noah's story to be included, as well as other amazing people who are making waves in the world of organ transplant through raising awareness and funds, and through research and medical discoveries.

My goal is to demonstrate that living life to the fullest is possible in adverse conditions, and that you can get through adversity if you frame it the right way. Swimming through adversity has worked for me. For others, it may be running, cycling, walking, singing, dancing, laughing, meditating, or even breathing through adversity. Whatever your approach, there is often a way through the most difficult challenges in life. You just have to find it.

In common with many organ transplant recipients, I also feel an obligation to publicize the case for organ transplant to encourage everyone to register as an organ donor. We have benefitted from this extraordinary gift of an organ - literally, the gift of life - from an anonymous donor and are asked for nothing in return.

Individually, we must find ways to express our gratitude for this unique gift. I believe that if people realize what can be accomplished, how lives can be saved, and changed by the simple action of agreeing to be an organ donor, more people would register. Each one additional registered organ donor has the potential to save up to eight lives.

Think about it and make an informed decision. And don't take your organs to Heaven.

Heaven knows we need them here.

# CHAPTER TWO: ESCAPE FROM ALCATRAZ

*"Since I've been warden, a few people have tried to escape.
Most of them have been recaptured; those that haven't have
been killed or drowned in the bay. No one has ever escaped
from Alcatraz. And no one ever will."*
— Warden in *Escape from Alcatraz* movie (1979)

**Five years post-transplant**

Zander's body briefly submerged as he jumped from the boat. As his head resurfaced, I could see the shock on his face. "Ahee, cold!" he spluttered. He grasped his bare arms, uncovered in the sleeveless wetsuit, and rubbed them vigorously as he bobbed up and down in the waves.

Splash! Riley hit the water a split second later, and she too surfaced with a look of horror. I had jumped from the boat moments before and turned around to face them, treading water as I watched them jump into the icy waters of San Francisco Bay.

"Dad, Dad, stay with me!" Riley cried, as she frantically oriented herself in the water.

"It's okay, guys," I said looking at their stricken faces. "You'll get used to it in a few minutes." I tried to sound reassuring, but I too was surprised by the surge of cold.

We were among a group of ten swimmers braving the open waters of San Francisco Bay on a one-and-a-half-mile swim from the notorious Alcatraz Island to the mainland. It was 8:00 a.m. on Sunday, May 12th, 2013, and the first seven swimmers were already in the water ahead of us, heading furiously towards the beach.

We turned and started swimming. The jagged assortment of buildings that made up the San Francisco skyline seemed far from our low vantage point. We were doing freestyle, and I could feel the cold water ripping across my face and hands. Visibility is awful in open-water, so I had to pause every ten or fifteen strokes to orient myself.

Any initial uncertainty felt by Zander and Riley quickly disappeared. They were both swimming as hard as they could.

Our kayaker guide hovered next to us; I was reassured that he was not going to let us out of his sight.

"Stay within a pool's length, or twenty-five yards, of each other at all times," Leslie Thomas, owner of the San Francisco-based group that organized the swim, told us.

"If you are moving away from the group, stop and wait for the slower swimmers." Good advice, but hard to follow for Zander and Riley. Their young, conditioned bodies, honed from pool-based practice, began steadily pulling away from me. I would go back into breaststroke to catch my breath, and then force myself into freestyle to catch up.

As soon as I caught them, they would turn in the water and speed off again, leaving me lagging. Our kayaker would paddle after them, making encouraging remarks like, "Keep it up," leaving me swimming behind. He turned around frequently. "Everything okay? Heart feeling strong? Breathing feeling good?" he would ask.

I nodded in acknowledgement. Yes, everything was absolutely fine. My breathing was heavier than I had anticipated, with the freezing water that encased my body adding to the sheer exertion of swimming in a wetsuit. But I felt physically strong and, most importantly, I felt spiritually indefatigable.

**Fifth anniversary**

"I want to swim from Alcatraz to celebrate my fifth anniversary," I had announced at dinner one Sunday evening the previous October. My wife, Julie, rolled her eyes, but said nothing. I could almost hear what she was thinking: oh great, another one of his crazy ideas. Zander and Riley looked up at me. They did not say anything either.

I was referring to the fifth anniversary of my double-lung transplant. Lung transplantation is complex, and recipients are typically judged on their post-operation survival at various stages: one year, three years, and five years. It was significant to reach the five-year mark and I wanted to celebrate the milestone.

Water has always had a strong allure for me. I enjoyed swimming as a competitive high school and college swimmer, but also as a recreational swimmer in lakes, ponds or oceans.

7

The previous summer, I had spoken to one of Zander and Riley's swimming coaches, who mentioned that she had competed in the "Alcatraz swim" a few years before. The Alcatraz swim! That really caught my imagination.

When I was fourteen, I participated in an Outward-Bound program in Scotland. The program's founder, John Ridgeway, had just completed the New York City Marathon before distance running became universally popular. In the same way as I heard about the marathon and felt compelled to compete – I ran the New York City Marathon on November 5th, 2000 – I felt that same compulsion to conquer this challenge.

I did some research online and found that there were several "vacation" companies (admittedly, not everyone's idea of a vacation) that organized swimming expeditions across San Francisco Bay. In my mind, it was conclusive: the open-water swim from Alcatraz would be the perfect way to celebrate my fifth anniversary.

"Think I can do it?" I asked to break the silence "It's not too far, just over a mile."

"Sure," Zander said cautiously. He paused cautiously. "But I want to do it too."

I was somewhat surprised. "But you're only thirteen. The water will be really cold, you know. Cold, with waves, currents, maybe sharks!"

"Sharks?" I had Riley's attention now and her eyes were bulging. She paused for a moment, ruminating. Then she said deliberately, "If Zander's doing it, can I do it too?"

"Rye", I reasoned, suddenly nervous. "You don't even like the waves. The water is really cold, and it's a long way in open water." Both Zander and Riley were strong competitive swimmers, but most of their experience was in heated swimming pools with lifeguards and lane ropes.

"But you just said it's only a mile," she fired back, fixing me with a hard stare. Her logic was indisputable. "I want to do it!"

"But Rye, you're only eleven!" I could feel my defenses crumbling. "It'll be cold, waves, currents, a tough swim…really!" I knew I was repeating myself. I had already lost the argument.

"I want to do it. With you and Zander," she confirmed emphatically. It was not a question anymore. Zander was nodding emphatically, encouraged by his sister's steely determination.

"Okay," I said, resignedly. I knew when I was beaten. "I'll look into it."

Initially, my idea was to swim in March, exactly five since my lung transplant, but Leslie Thomas advised us to wait until May when the water would be several degrees warmer.

"How old are your kids?" she asked, when I contacted her. Leslie's website stated that she had won the Tampa Bay swim marathon in 2005, so she was no swimming slouch. She had been involved in open-water swimming for fifteen years and had organized dozens of Alcatraz swims.

"Thirteen and eleven." Their ages sounded young as I said them out loud. "They're really good swimmers, though." I added.

"What's their open-water experience?" She sounded hesitant. Clearly, the last thing she wanted was a group of inexperienced swimmers getting into difficulty in unpredictable waters.

"Well," I paused for a moment to think. Truthfully, none of us had a very convincing open-water swimming pedigree. I had swum in open water events when I was younger, but not in the last three decades. The children had swum in the Caribbean on vacation in Mexico the year before, but I was reluctant to mention that as the basis of our experience.

Instead, I settled for, "Living in Colorado, there're not so many opportunities for ocean swimming. However, they've both swum in lakes during triathlons, they train in a pool several times a week," I paused. "And they're pretty tough kids."

Leslie seemed satisfied. "Take a look at the training plans on the website," she suggested.

The twelve-week training plan set out a gradual build-up, starting with three swims per week, with steadily increasing distance and intensity. "Swim at least three times per week, at least a mile each time. Ideally, one swim in open water, preferably under choppy conditions."

We started training. Zander and Riley were already on a swim team and had regular practices at 4:30 to 6:00 p.m. every day after school. Usually, I would take the opportunity to swim myself while they were in practice, so I could easily chalk up 1,500 meters in an hour. The goal was to swim a mile (sixty-four lengths of a twenty-five-meter pool) in forty-five minutes.

As the weeks went on, I enjoyed the excuse I had created for myself to be in the water almost every day and trained diligently. I swam from January until April and felt confident that I was in good shape for the upcoming challenge.

It is likely that physical exercise contributes to recovery in lung transplant recipients. After the operation, I exercised as recommended by the rehabilitation center, and often a lot more. When I completed a sprint-distance triathlon after thirteen months with my new lungs, I knew I could get my health and fitness back.

## Swim day

The swim day started early. Zander, Riley, Julie and I were awake by 6:00 a.m. in our hotel room close to Fisherman's Wharf. We had flown in the day before from Colorado. This was a day we had been looking forward to for months. Our wetsuits were neatly laid out on the floor, and we pulled them on as we wolfed down mouthfuls of omelets and toast.

"Remember to eat a warm breakfast the morning of the swim," the instructions had said. "Food = fuel = energy = warmth. Get a good night's sleep the night before. Expect to be tired on Sunday night."

With jackets, hats, and a bag of dry clothes, we left the hotel room and hailed a taxi. It was not far to the meeting point at the north end of Van Ness Drive, but we did not want to expend an ounce of extra energy to get there.

We were the first ones at the meeting point at 7:00 a.m. and savored the view out across the grey waters of San Francisco Bay as the sun came up. There were a handful of joggers making their ways around the walkways at Aquatic Park. I put my pack against a tree and started a warm-up run along the walkway next to the sandy beach.

My wetsuit felt tight as I ran, but my breathing was slow and steady. I felt I had to run to prepare for the exertion of the swim.

With my transplanted lungs, it takes longer to open the airways, so oxygen can flow easily. I reached the end of the walkway, turned around and ran back, striding faster and faster as I neared the end. I slowed down, and stopped, panting heavily.

"Hi, I'm Mark," said a man with an outstretched hand. "I'm your kayaker this morning." He was in his early fifties, shorn hair, and a wide grin. He was dressed in a waterproof jacket beneath a life jacket and carried a luminous green kayak in his right hand. We talked for a few minutes, and I introduced him to Julie, Zander and Riley. He told me he had done the crossing dozens of times, and that we just needed to follow his directions, and we would easily make it to shore. I was glad of his experience.

Four or five other people arrived, wetsuits in their hands and kit bags over their shoulders. There were three men, all in their forties or fifties, lean and fit, with smiles on their faces. A tall middle-aged lady sported a sweatshirt that stated, "Member of the 100,000 Yard Club." A quick mental calculation told me that if there were 1,760 yards in a mile, several swims of at least fifty-six miles featured in her swimming past.

A fit-looking lady in her thirties told us she had done the crossing multiple times and loved it. When she met Zander and Riley, she commented about how she was sure that no one in her family would ever accompany her on the swim.

Two latecomers arrived, a man of Indian origin in his thirties, wearing what he called his "Farmer John's" cut-off wetsuit. As he got ready, he confided that he worked for Google in nearby Mountain View and had been preparing for the swim by lunchtime training in one of the company's jet-stream pools.

The last arrival was a seventeen-year-old youth who was conspicuous by the absence of a wetsuit. Later, we would learn that he crossed in less than thirty minutes. He confidently adjusted his goggles as we gathered on the grass bank around Leslie for the pre-swim briefing.

I checked my watch. Drug time. I had carefully adjusted the timing of my morning dose of my twice daily immunosuppressant drug, tacrolimus. I quickly swallowed the capsules with a gulp of water.

There were ten swimmers on the grassy slope at 7:15 a.m. that morning. I stood with the others, suited up and eager with anticipation, with Zander and Riley on either side of me.

"It's only a five-minute walk to the Hyde Street Pier, where we will take the boat," said Leslie.

She inked a large number on the backs of each swimmer's hands with a massive marker pen: we were numbers eight, nine and ten.

"You have all been assigned to your kayaks, so stay close as you swim," she reminded us.

"You will be swimming across two rivers, one flowing from the Golden Gate Bridge from west to east. Once you cross that, there is a second river flowing in the opposite direction from east to west. Watch the currents and keep sight of your target building on the skyline. Listen to your kayaker. He is your guide. And don't worry, we'll all watch for you, so you are perfectly safe. There will always be at least one pair of eyes on you at all times." She paused as she looked around at the group.

"As long as the pair of eyes is not from below!" smirked one of the swimmers. We all grinned. Riley looked round at me, her eyes wide. She knew it was not serious, but probably not the best joke for her right then.

"Okay, let's go," continued Leslie. "Take only whatever is essential on board, your jacket, swim cap, and goggles. Be ready to swim at 8:15 a.m. – jump time!"

We walked around the walkway at the water's edge of Aquatic Park to Hyde Street Pier and on to the thirty-foot support boat that would take us out to the island. It only seemed like minutes of leaving the pier that we were motoring out into the open bay and towards the mesmerizing, forbidding island of Alcatraz.

## The Rock

The allure of Alcatraz is undeniable. "The Rock" was developed with facilities for a lighthouse, a military fortification, a military prison and, most famously, a federal prison from 1933 to 1963. While well-known criminals such as Al Capone served time on Alcatraz, most of the 1,500 prisoners were not high-profile. Alcatraz served as the federal prison system's prison. If a convict did not behave at another institution, he could be sent to Alcatraz, where the structured daily routine was designed to subdue the toughest inmates.

During its twenty-nine years as a prison, the penitentiary never logged any successful escapes. Potential escapees were either shot dead or assumed drowned in the frigid waters of San Francisco Bay. Prison records tell us that thirty-six prisoners were involved in escape attempts. Of those, seven were shot and killed, two drowned, five unaccounted for, and the others were recaptured. Two prisoners made it off the island but were returned; one in 1945 and one in 1962.

In 1962, three would-be escapees disappeared from their cells in an intricate escape attempt - portrayed in the 1979 movie *Escape from Alcatraz*, starring Clint Eastwood. Although no evidence was found that the prisoners died in their attempt, they are officially listed as "missing, presumed drowned." The FBI subsequently found wooden paddles and parts of a raft made from raincoats, but it is generally thought likely that they died in the attempt. In all the intervening years, no one has ever surfaced claiming to be, or even to have seen, the escapees.

As the support boat pulled up alongside the island, Julie pointed out the fading sign that threatens approaching boats: *"Warning. Persons Procuring Or Concealing Escape Of Prisoners Are Subject To Prosecution And Imprisonment."*

Although the sign is a remnant of the penitentiary days, swimmers are not permitted to go ashore on the island, which is protected federal property. We were going to be jumping from the boat directly adjacent to the island. Swimming expeditions are required to get special permission to make the crossing. A swimmer risks arrest for undertaking an unauthorized aquatic jaunt in the bay.

I looked back at the skyline. San Francisco was just a mile-and-a-half away. The proximity was striking. It has been said that prisoners on Alcatraz were often tantalized by the sounds of normal city life – music, laughter, maddeningly close just across the water but, at the same time, as good as a million miles away.

13

Was the shore that close? I felt a rush of exhilaration as Leslie began instructing the swimmers to jump. One of the other swimmers, a man probably ten years older than me, was grinning as he adjusted his goggles. As he got up to walk to the boat's stern, he turned and said, "This really is a great thing to do. Enjoy it!" He plunged overboard. Seconds later, Zander, Riley and I joined him.

The three of us swam together for the first twenty minutes, alternating between freestyle and breaststroke. Mark continued to encourage us from the kayak. Zander and Riley had acclimatized to the cold and began to enjoy the sensation of being tossed around in the water. I could see their bright green swim caps just in front of me and hear their high-pitched voices as they bantered back and forth. I was concentrating on my swimming, pulling slow steady strokes, and aiming for the buildings silhouetted on the skyline.

The fact that the kids chatted with each other as they swam, despite the cold, the waves, and the currents, seemed incredible. I could hear Riley's higher pitched voice floating in the air. Was she actually singing? I grinned to myself in the water.

After the swim, Riley told us that she started singing to herself to keep her confidence up. Demi Lovato, one of her favorite artists, had a recent song called *"Heart Attack"*. *"If I ever did that, I think I'd have a heart attack"* went the words. Riley changed them for the swim to suit her circumstances: *"If I ever did that, I think I'd have a shark attack!"* she sang as she swam.

Thirty minutes in, Zander and Riley were getting impatient. "C'mon, Dad!" they would shout as they waited for me to catch up. I would break into freestyle to catch them but, as soon as I reached them, they would surge forward and leave me behind again.

"Dad, swim a bit faster!" they shouted. I felt like a stage performer doing his best to entertain a restless audience, only to be continuously heckled. "Wow," I remember thinking to myself. "Tough crowd!"

Before the swim, I would joke with Zander and Riley about sharks. "Don't be the last swimmer in the group," I said. "It's always the last swimmer who gets eaten!" About this time in the swim, I realized that I was the last swimmer in the group. It would serve me right for those stupid jokes, I admonished myself.

Sharks might not be the only hazard. A couple of months earlier, I read a news article about the annual *Escape from Alcatraz* triathlon. Not for the timid, the first leg is the swim from the island to the shore, followed by an eighteen-mile bike ride and a hilly eight-mile run. Over 1,700 athletes competed in the event. Tragically, a forty-six-year-old competitor suffered a fatal cardiac arrest during the event's swim portion. The report did not confirm the cause of death but speculated that he suffered from an underlying heart issue that was exacerbated by the sudden plunge into cold water, a so-called "pre-existing condition."

Hmm..., I thought. I had just turned forty-six. I could possibly be described as having something of a pre-existing condition too.

"No one has died before in the thirty-three-year history of the event," the race director was quoted as saying; very reassuring.

I felt the first twinge of cramp in my left leg. I kept swimming, determined to ignore it. We were almost three-quarters of the way across the bay now. The skyline was much clearer, and I could make out the eroding Ghirardelli sign from the old chocolate factory.

Distances in open-water swimming are deceiving. It seems as if you are getting nowhere, as the scenery does not change. You must trust that you are still moving steadily through the water and getting closer to dry land.

There is something soothing and relaxing, even spiritual, about swimming in open-water. The waves gently move you up and down, and you feel the silkiness of the water on your exposed skin. The huge expanse of water can be mentally overpowering, especially if you dwell on how deep the water is beneath you and how endless on all sides. More than just being a physical experience, open-water swimming is mental and spiritual for me.

A couple of times I flipped over and did a few strokes of backstroke. The sensation was amazing. Out in the open, there is no ceiling, no flags, nor lanes markers that are found in a swimming pool. All I could see was the vast expanse of sky.

The images were all very well but, from a practical viewpoint, I was unable to tell where I was heading so, after a few strokes, I flipped back onto my front. In the vastness of San Francisco Bay that morning, I reveled in the energy of the ocean and the gift of breath that buoyed me on this first thrilling swim adventure.

I had swum in open-water before, although not recently. When I was thirteen, I swam part-way across the bay at Fraserburgh, Scotland, where I grew up. The bay is about two miles across, but you probably swim three miles once you adjust for the tide. I did not make it on that attempt and had to be pulled out of the water about three-quarters of the way across by the Fraserburgh Lifeboat crew, shivering and near hypothermic.

The following year, I tried again and, this time, made the successful crossing, along with a handful of friends from the local swimming club. The water temperature of the North Sea – never rising above the mid-fifties[1] – was about the same as the year before and broadly comparable to the north-west Pacific, so still a chilly experience. Back then, like today, I found the challenge of open-water swimming irresistible.

Today, with the expanse of San Francisco Bay before me, my transplanted lungs were giving me the nourishment my body needed. Lungs are complex organs. Essentially, they take a gas that your body needs to get rid of - carbon dioxide - and exchange it for a gas that your body inherently needs - oxygen. It's that process of "oxygen exchange," almost impossible five years before, which my new lungs still find challenging. I was consciously thankful for every breath.

**Successful escape**

Zander and Riley were much farther ahead of me now, a lot more than twenty-five yards. Mark stayed closer to them

---

1    About 12°C

than to me but kept looking back. We were really close to the entrance to the Aquatic Park enclosure, around five hundred yards away.

Julie was onboard the support boat and commented afterwards how Leslie did a continuous safety count of swimmers, identified by their bright green swim caps. "One, two three," she would count. "Then over there, four and five, then six, seven and eight. Two already finished."

Julie was also aware that this second Sunday in May when she was onboard a boat watching her family bob in the open sea was also Mother's Day. Not exactly the chocolates and flowers one might expect, she thought wryly.

After another ten minutes, a second kayaker appeared from the entrance. He had finished escorting one of the other swimmers and had headed back out to support the swimmers who were still coming in. He paddled alongside Zander and Riley and encouraged them to swim alongside him all the way to the beach. Mark stayed back with me as the kids surged forward with their new escort.

Cramp spread suddenly from my left leg to my right leg. Both legs locked, and I knew I could not swim through it any more. I needed to drink fresh water in the next few minutes or I would be contorted in agony. I signaled to Mark that I needed some help. He was next to me in an instant. "Cramp!" was all I could grimace as the pain shot through both legs. I grabbed the back of his kayak, as he called the support boat on his radio.

"I need to get out," I gasped.

"But you're so close!" he shouted in dismay. The entrance to Aquatic Park was only two hundred yards away. As the support boat powered up next to me, I grabbed the rail at the back, and hauled myself, with no help from my legs, onto the back of the boat.

Julie knew immediately what the problem was and thrust a bottle of water into my hand. "Drink!" she yelled.

I tilted my head back and emptied the whole bottle in two or three gulps. Almost instantaneously, the cramp that had hijacked the muscles in my legs eased and then evaporated. I pulled on my swim cap back on, adjusted my goggles, and jumped off the back of the boat again. I had been out of the water for less than five minutes. This time, in contrast to our initial entry, the water felt deliciously warm and welcoming.

By now, Zander and Riley were already on the beach within the Aquatic Park boundary. I swam determinedly towards the shore and focusing on the finish. A sea lion turned lazily in the water about twenty yards in front of me, reminding me of the jokes we had make about sharks before the swim.

The shark attack folklore was probably fueled by prison guards who would tell inmates that the waters were shark-infested to deter escape attempts. While the presence of sharks has never been proven, the cold water and strong currents are real and, equally, would have been a significant deterrent to would-be escapees.

The sandy shore was just in front of me. I tried to put my feet down, but it was still out of my depth. Two, three more strokes. I tried again, and I could feel the gritty bottom. I pulled forward, then stood up in the water and waded onto dry land. I could see Zander and Riley further along the beach.

I was struck by the silence and peace of this sunny Sunday morning and, seized by a sudden surge of energy, ran across the beach towards my children, water oozing from my wetsuit. I was shivering wildly, but I didn't feel cold. I felt hugely elated.

"Zander, Rye! Great job! You did it. We all did it!" I grabbed them, cold and damp, and hugged them tightly. The swim had taken us just over an hour.

They let me hold them for a few moments.

"Dad!" Riley pulled back and looked up at me sternly. "Dad, next year…" she paused. "Next year, you'll need to have your own kayak!"

"Okay," I said, grinning. "Okay."

Like I said before, tough crowd.

Riley and Zander celebrating their escape from Alcatraz. May 2013

Zander, Gavin and Riley after escape from Alcatraz swim. May 2013

# CHAPTER THREE: THAT OXYGEN THING

*"Everything will be okay in the end. If it's not okay, it's not the end."*

- John Lennon

## Slow marathon time

The family doctor politely listened to my complaints. A persistent dry cough, I see. More tired than usual, yes, I understand. Some weight loss? Anything unusual in your activities, she inquired solicitously?

Her demeanor changed when I told her that I had just arrived back from a weekend in the United States – I was living in London at the time – where I had travelled to compete in the New York City Marathon. My marathon time had been quite a bit slower than I had anticipated, I pointed out; an unremarkable five hours for the twenty-six-mile road race.

The doctor was nonplused. After confirming that I was not asthmatic and a non-smoker, she shrugged.

"Perhaps try to rest more?" she suggested.

It was hard to argue with her assessment. I was both relieved and a little embarrassed. I was relieved that I did not have symptoms of a serious underlying condition and embarrassed at having wasted the doctor's time. I was thirty-four years old and had always enjoyed good health, so nothing suggested that anything untoward was going on. Over the next few months, the annoying cough lessened, but never really went away.

I have always enjoyed athletic activities. I have never smoked and generally maintained a healthy and positive lifestyle. At high school at Fraserburgh Academy, I swam in the local youth swimming club, usually at 7:00 a.m. six mornings a week. I spent my final two years at Gordonstoun School in Morayshire, Scotland, where I held the swimming record for the one hundred-meter freestyle.

The boarding school had its very own twenty-five-meter swimming pool on campus but, for arcane reasons, the pool building was usually locked and inaccessible. I would frequently jog back to my boarding house after afternoon rugby practice, pick up my swim suit and towel, then jog the extra mile over to the swimming pool building. To get to the water, I had to sneak through the gym, go up to the unlocked spectators' gallery, climb the railings and drop down in the semi-darkness of the pool-side. Even as the daylight was fading, I could usually get two or three clandestine swimming workouts per week. As they say, necessity is the mother of invention.

As an undergraduate at the University of Dundee in Scotland, swimming was my main sport. I competed against other Scottish university teams every year of the four-year degree program. My best events were freestyle and butterfly. I enjoyed competing but, more than anything, I loved the regular workouts and the feeling of being physically fit and strong.

As I moved through my twenties and thirties, I had less time to find swimming pools and turned to longer-distance running. I competed in over fifty ten kilometer and half-marathons events. Among the many highlights were completing the London Marathon in 1998 and 1999, as well as the New York City Marathon in 2000.

While I ran well in both London marathons, I felt disappointed with my pace in the New York City Marathon. In the London event, I had trained consistently and finished in four hours, but New York took me a long five hours. In the last few weeks of training, I had the nagging feeling that something wasn't quite right. The final two miles of the New Yok City Marathon was through the fall colors of Central Park and I finished at a near-walking pace. On crossing the line, I could not stop coughing, despite being wrapped in a shiny space blanket for warmth. I had trouble controlling the cough for the next few hours.

Julie and I had been contemplating a move from London. Julie is an American citizen who grew up in Colorado. We decided that the outdoor lifestyle, the open space, and sunshine would be a healthy environment for our family. I was confident that my skills in accounting and business would make employment feasible in the United States. Zander was three and Riley was one year old at the time.

As a British citizen, I needed authorization to move to the United States, even with an American spouse. I filled out the paperwork and applied for permanent resident status (the coveted "green card") at the American Embassy in London in early September 2001. Processing delays were inevitably caused by the events of September 11th, but I received the required permission a month later. We were cleared for take-off. In February 2002, we packed all our possessions into boxes, called the moving company, and left our rented flat in north-west London, bound for Denver, Colorado.

We initially rented a two-bedroom apartment in a Denver suburb – exactly double the floor space and half the monthly rent of our flat in London – and I kept exercising as normal. Around the end of 2002, I still had the persistent dry cough. It is difficult to pinpoint exactly when it started, as I often attributed it to the symptoms of a lingering cold. But it was always there and slightly worse when I went jogging.

Periodically, I would go and see a doctor and explain my symptoms. On taking my medical history – generally good health, a never-smoker, no family history of respiratory issues, and no obvious environmental exposure issues – the doctor would invariably conclude that I was suffering from one of two things: allergies or asthma. The explanation was always inadequate as I had not previously suffered from any allergies, although a frequent retort was that late onset allergies were not uncommon. Asthma was always a tempting diagnosis, as the symptoms fitted the complaint: a dry, exercise-induced cough. Having moved recently from London, it was also tempting to at least partly attribute the cough to my body's reaction to the aridity and altitude of Colorado.

But the cough did not clear up. It persisted, day and night, week in, week out, summer and winter. The symptoms were annoying, and not just to me. Even so, it was inconceivable at the time that a time-bomb lung disease was lurking in my chest.

22

By January 2004, my cough had become such a source of irritation that I could not carry on a conversation, make a phone call, or attend a business meeting without a coughing fit. Colleagues would hand me a glass of water or offer cough drops. I would maintain a pretense that it was just some minor temporary irritant and laugh it off.

Julie and I decided to make an appointment with a lung specialist to get to the bottom of the problem once and for all. I made an appointment to see a pulmonologist at a nationally-renowned pulmonary clinic in Denver. I confidently turned up for my appointment expecting a simple remedy to the troublesome cough.

Before I saw the pulmonologist, I had my first exposure to two standard respiratory diagnostic tools. First was the chest x-ray and second was the spirometry test. Once the x-ray was done, a spirometry technician patiently led me though the steps of blowing into the tube to collect lung function readings. Little did I realize that this short introduction in 2004 was the start of my lifelong association with the world of spirometry. My current understanding is that despite advances in many areas of pulmonary medicine, the humble spirometry machine, which measures volume and flow of air, is still one of the most reliable measures of lung health.

The pulmonologist listened to my complaint and took a detailed medical history. He asked about my overall health (good), my parents' and brothers' health (also good), any negative environmental factors I may have been exposed to (his examples included asbestos from a ship building yard or dust from a coal mine), as well as any smoking history. Everything was negative. I confirmed no history of health problems, no family health problems, no ship yards or coal mines, and definitely no smoking. The spirometry readings told him that my predicted lung function was lower than expected for a person of my age. The x-ray seemed clear.

Being a smoker would allow him to pinpoint the source of my complaint, so he again pressed to see if I really was a non-smoker.

"You're sure you've never smoked?" he asked for a third time, almost hopefully.

"No, never."

"Hmm, that a pity."

A pity? How could something I had never done have any bearing on my condition? Maybe it would be easier if I started to smoke to get the benefit from stopping, I thought to myself.

The pulmonologist was literally scratching his head. At the end of the consultation, he hesitatingly concluded that I had a nasal irritation, but he did not seem very confident in his diagnosis. I remember saying to him that a cough was symptomatic of an underlying condition and not a condition in itself. He agreed but could not shed any light on why I was still coughing. I left with a prescription for a saline nasal rinse and a feeling of relief that at least the cough was not the sign of any serious condition. If it had been, the pulmonologist would have found it – surely.

## Major league pneumonia

Two days after my appointment, I felt terrible. I had flu-like symptoms, with aching muscles, a raging temperature, and a horrific cough. I lay in bed all weekend and into the next week. By Tuesday morning, I began coughing up rust-colored sputum. Julie drove me to the hospital.

I didn't have much experience with emergency rooms. I broke my collar bone when I was fifteen years old and remember sitting waiting for medical attention for a several hours before being seen, so I expected a long wait. But this time was different. As I presented myself at the front desk of the Emergency Room (ER), the receptionist asked me what was wrong. I said that I was having some trouble breathing. She slipped an oxygen saturation meter onto my middle finger and looked at the reading. She immediately reached for the telephone. Moments later, an orderly appeared with a wheel chair and asked me to sit down. I was wheeled straight through to a treatment room. Given the stories of people waiting for hours in the ER, I realized that being seen so quickly was not a good sign.

It turned out that I had pneumonia. I was surprised. Surely pneumonia was a condition for older people? Although I was worried by the diagnosis, I also felt relieved as it may be the underlying cause of my persistent cough. I was admitted to the hospital for one night. I ended up staying for seven days.

I was inundated by the same round of medical questions I had answered many times before: were there any lung issues in my family; did I have any potentially harmful environmental exposure; did I keep birds? All my answers were no, no, and no. I could not provide a good reason why I had contracted pneumonia.

The doctor told Julie that I had, in his words, "major league" pneumonia and that if I had been older, my recovery would have been serious doubt. Fortunately, my relative youth and good overall health played in my favor. While in the hospital, I experienced my first use of supplemental oxygen and two consecutive rounds of robust antibiotics. My diagnosis on discharge from the hospital was "community-acquired pneumococcal pneumonia."

**Holmesian search**

I was weak from the illness but felt relieved that it had been treated successfully. The doctor predicted that I would make a full recovery, so I was confident that the worst was over. This episode must have been the culmination of the coughing, and I would soon be back to normal, I thought.

But the cough gradually returned. I kept thinking that it was a remnant from the pneumonia, but the weeks passed, and the cough stayed. By July, I decided to try the same specialist clinic again. I made an appointment, but with a different pulmonologist this time.

The doctor somewhat was laconic but exuded competence. He had already reviewed my medical notes and came straight to the point. "Let's get a CT (computed tomography) scan," he said tersely. The consultation lasted less than five minutes.

Two weeks later I was back in front of him, having had the CT scan. I was nervous this time. Something was obviously bothering him. He did not have the same air of confidence as before. He looked at me with his dark eyes. "There's something on your CT scan. I'm not sure what it is. It's unusual."

"What do you mean, unusual?" I asked with trepidation.

"Well, it's just unusual," he said. "I'm perplexed."

"How can you be perplexed?" I shot back incredulously. "You are the expert in this area. How can you be perplexed?"

"I am," he said, with a shrug. "I recommend a lung biopsy. Both lungs are diseased, but the right one is worse than the left. I can arrange it in the next ten days, if you like."

If I like? What choice did I have? This was much worse than I expected. I felt my stomach churn. A biopsy? I scarcely knew what that meant.

"The biopsy itself is nothing to worry about," the doctor said. He explained that the surgeon would make a small incision in my chest through my ribs to extract a sample from the diseased lung for further analysis. The hole in the lung would quickly close by itself.

"After the procedure, you will be in hospital for one night, maybe two. You will be uncomfortable for about four weeks afterwards," he cautioned.

I left the doctor's office in a daze. What on earth was wrong? I couldn't think straight as I made my way to my car. None of it made any sense.

An online search at home told me that a biopsy was "a medical removal of cells or tissues from a living subject to determine the presence of a disease." That sounded serious. I could feel nervousness running up my spine. After discussing it with Julie, I decided to go ahead as soon as possible. If there was bad news, I wanted to know, so treatment could start. I called the doctor's office and scheduled the procedure for the day before my thirty-eighth birthday.

It was recommended that Julie and I meet with the biopsy surgeon in advance of the procedure, so we set up an appointment. As we were waiting for him, one of his associates came into our room and said, "The doctor will be with you in a moment. By the way, I've seen your CT scan. It doesn't look good!" With that, he ducked out of the room.

I couldn't believe his bluntness. Doesn't look good? What did that mean? Did that mean I was going to die? Julie was sitting beside me and burst into tears.

The surgeon was more circumspect. He showed us the CT scan without drama. I had the vague knowledge that a scan is a representation of density. Bones are dense, so x-rays will not pass through as readily as soft tissue. It is a negative image, so dense material, such as bone, is lighter, while less dense material, such as soft tissue, is darker. The dark shading between the white-colored ribs should have been clear, showing healthy lung tissue.

But my scan looked like a sinister version of van Gogh's *Starry Night*, with light asteroid-like dots over the dark background. There was no doubt why he wanted to investigate.

The biopsy day came and went. The pain killers kept me comfortable, while the drainage tube on right side on my lower back emitted a red colored liquid. The first two days passed, and I was ready to go home. Each morning, one of the doctors would enter my room at 6:00 a.m. and look at the drainage box. He would give it a prod, then shake his head. "There's still output. Maybe one more day."

One more day passed. Then another. Then another. I was getting more impatient by each passing day. Why wouldn't they let me go home? Why wouldn't the wound in my side stop bleeding? I had been expecting a hospital stay of one or two nights, but I eventually spent ten nights in hospital until the doctors were satisfied that the bleeding was under control.

## Idio-what?

A week after the biopsy, I spoke to the doctor from my hospital room to ask for the results. I realized it was possible I had lung cancer.

"Well, we know what is wrong with you," he said. 'It's quite rare."

"What is it?" I asked anxiously.

"Well, it's a condition called idiopathic pleuroparenchymal fibroelastosis. Or IPPFE for short," he added helpfully.

"Idio-what?" I said. I was swimming in medical terminology. It was also ironic that I had a lung disease diagnosis, the name of which I struggled to say in one breath.

"It's idiopathic," he said. "That just means we don't know where it comes from. Your condition is a form of pulmonary fibrosis, which means the lung tissue is hardened and scarred. That is why you are having a hard time breathing and probably why you are coughing.

"What can you do about it?"

The doctor sidestepping the question. "I'm going to refer you to the real expert in this area at the interstitial lung disease program. You'll be in good hands."

As he rung off, I sank back in my hospital chair and tried to absorb the information. The medical diagnosis seemed surreal. I must be in a bad dream. I looked at the name of the disease – I had scribbled it down while the doctor spelled it out. It was forty-one letters long. How could I be suffering from some ultra-rare condition with such a ridiculously long name? The bottom line was it was not good. I had a degenerative lung disease. It would take more than another round of antibiotics to clear it up.

Julie told me later that, after I called her, she went straight to a computer and searched the diagnosis. The results made her collapse onto the floor, sobbing and crying.

At least the diagnosis explained why the right side of my chest was still bleeding. As I understood it, the surgeon had reached into the most diseased area of my right lung to get a tissue sample for analysis. As the lung tissue had hardened, it had a difficult job repairing itself after the invasive biopsy, so the lung kept bleeding long after the doctors expected it to heal.

After ten days, I was discharged from the hospital and went home. Again, I hoped that the worst was behind me and I could get back to normal. The earliest available follow-up appointment with the expert in interstitial lung disease was scheduled for two weeks later.

When we met with interstitial lung disease expert, he informed us that there weren't many treatment options. The best we could do, he suggested, was to keep an eye on it and hope that the condition did not deteriorate any further. He did not recommend any further therapy or medications.

Julie and I left the appointment feeling dejected. We still hoped that there was a chance that the mysterious condition would clear itself up with some act of spontaneous healing. It was October 2004.

## Head-scratching

As 2004 gave way to 2005 and then to 2006, I still had the persistent cough, but generally convinced myself that I felt fine. But by 2006, I was noticeably losing weight. I had never had a weight issue before and usually maintained my body at a consistent one hundred and seventy-five[2] pounds all my adult life. Now my weight had dwindled to around one hundred and sixty[3] pounds. I found that it was harder to maintain a regular eating schedule.

Not surprisingly, I had reached a point where I didn't know what to do any more. Any doctors I consulted adopted a Fabian policy of watchful waiting. I felt that I had exhausted the conventional medical options.

I was at the point of avoiding people I knew, as they invariably commented on my emaciated look. In public, I tried to smile and shrug it off; in private, I was tired and miserable. When you are not in full health, you make unconscious adjustments to your lifestyle. We cut out all trips to the mountains, where we used to enjoy hiking, and replaced them with slow walks to the local park. There was a gradual creep of doing fewer and fewer physical activities.

Then it happened. I couldn't take it anymore. Julie and I had just returned to Denver from a sea-level business trip. I found that whenever I went to sea level, I felt better – hardly surprisingly, as it was lack of available oxygen that was contributing to my sensation of feeling so unwell.

It was Saturday, October 6th, 2007. We planned to have a leisurely day at home with the kids. I remember sinking down

---

2    80kg
3    73kg

into a chair and saying to Julie that I didn't feel well. Julie suggested that we go out for breakfast and that maybe I would feel better. I agreed and let her drive. Once we got the restaurant, I could barely touch my food. My head sank onto the table. I was literally gasping for breath. I felt I was suffocating.

Julie bundled me out of the restaurant and into the car. She drove to the hospital where I had the lung biopsy performed three years before. As before, when I went to the ER with pneumonia in 2004, the receptionist measured my oxygen saturation level and I was immediately escorted to a treatment room.

The doctors put me on supplemental oxygen, took me through to radiology for a chest x-ray, and asked me the list of familiar questions about health history and environmental exposure. They could see the lung biopsy from my medical records.

Several different doctors came in and out of my room and all asked the same questions. They were relieved to see that my oxygen saturation level rose from the low eighties into the high nineties with the supplemental oxygen. I was extremely hungry. Someone brought a sandwich and I devoured it in a couple of bites. I was surprised as I had not been hungry for the last several months. A doctor explained that the oxygen had probably triggered my appetite. In my oxygen-starved state, my body was focusing on breathing, not eating. Now that I had enough oxygen, I was suddenly ravenous.

I was admitted to the hospital's pulmonary unit. Whatever was wrong was not a quick-fix. I felt much better with the oxygen, but I was becoming very worried. What did it mean to have supplemental oxygen? How long would I have to use it? Would it repair my damaged lungs?

None of the doctors seemed willing to answer any questions. They still seemed to be gathering information. When I was weighed, I was surprised to see that my weight had fallen to one hundred and twenty-five pounds, which meant that I had lost almost a third of my body weight. I could tell that I was skinny, even emaciated, as I sat there in my hospital gown. It was not a pleasant realization.

30

We knew that the doctors were about to tell us what they thought was going on. Around mid-morning the next day, three doctors came into my room. The leader, a young, shaven-headed man, summarized the findings: my lungs were in bad shape, my breathing was impaired, and I was going to have to use the supplemental oxygen for some time.

"What do you mean by "some time?" I asked cautiously.

"Well, you are a chronic case. That means that you will need to use the oxygen for as long as you need it."

"You mean, forever?"

He had trouble looking me in the eye. He nodded. "We think the next step…" He paused and looked away. He was clearly uncomfortable with his ineluctable conclusion.

"The next step…" he continued, "…is to talk to the transplant people."

I was speechless. "You mean lung transplant?" was what I wanted to say, but I couldn't get any sound out of my mouth. I looked at Julie. Her eyes had filled with tears. This was the first time I had ever thought about the possibility of a lung transplant. Questions flooded my mind. I didn't know where to start. How, where, when…? I felt a wave of fear. Julie told me later that she had already considered the possibility of lung transplant and was more prepared for it.

"How long before…?" my question tailed off. The lead doctor anticipated what I was asking.

"Probably six months," he said, looking out the window. "We can do it here. We have a great transplant team", he said. He suddenly seemed anxious to wind up the meeting.

"I will set you up with an appointment for an evaluation in the next couple of weeks. They will be able to answer all your questions. There is no reason to stay here. You can go home. We will arrange home oxygen supplies for you."

All three left the room. Not for the first time, I fought to control my feelings of panic and confusion. But there was nothing left to do there, so Julie and I packed up my things, transferred my cannula to the portable oxygen tank, and headed home.

**That oxygen thing**

October and November 2007 passed slowly as I waited to take the first steps towards becoming a lung transplant candidate. I was on supplementary oxygen twenty-four hours a day.

After I was discharged from the hospital, an oxygen supply truck pulled up outside our house and the driver unloaded tanks of oxygen. The oxygen tanks made me very scared. I knew that it meant that I was now fully dependent on supplementary oxygen. The oxygen was literally keeping me alive, but I had no idea when I would be rid of it. I could not go very far while fettered to the oxygen tank. The oxygen company had provided a unit called a concentrator that converted normal air into oxygen, and it hummed loudly from the center of the main floor of our house. It represented an ugly reminder of my predicament.

After the referral, we had to wait for an appointment with one of the specialized lung transplant pulmonologists to talk through options. I spent a lot of time contemplating my situation and the very real prospect of a lung transplant. I had read that it was not uncommon for patients to perish while waiting for an organ transplant, which exacerbated my feelings of nervousness. It seemed obvious that I was a good candidate for a lung transplant. I didn't see why I wouldn't be accepted, as I was perfectly healthy apart from the lung condition.

Just before the 2007 November Thanksgiving holiday, Julie and I had an appointment at the hospital's lung transplant clinic. I was looking forward to this meeting as it promised to answer a lot of our questions and hopefully set out road map for going forward.

At the appointment, we met with a transplant pulmonologist. He answered our questions, such as, "how do you get the lungs out of there?" and "how long would the operation take?" and "would I get a general anesthetic?" and, of course, "one lung or two?"

He answered breezily. "We just pop up the hood and change them over," he said, while making a slicing gesture with his hand across his chest.

"It takes eight to ten hours," he added, nodding enthusiastically.

"A general anesthetic?"

"Yes."

"One lung or two?

"Could be either. In your case, probably two."

There was also the six-hour thing.

"When it happens, we will need to move quickly," he said. There is only about a six-hour window between obtaining donor organs and getting them into a recipient's body."

As many donors are victims of motor vehicle accidents, stroke, and heart attack victims, it means recovering the lungs, dispatching surgeons from the lung transplant team to pick them up and deliver them to the hospital and the recipient. All within six hours.

"We have done it in nine hours, but that is really the upper limit. We prefer to do it within six," he said.

"And there are other potential complications," he went on. "You will be more susceptible to certain forms of cancer, there may be damage to your kidneys, and there is the constant threat of rejection."

He paused for breath to give us time to absorb everything. "Transplant is not a cure," he said. "It simply exchanges one set of health problems for another."

"Would I get my life back?" I asked. He looked at me for a few moments, considering a response.

"Yes," he conceded at last. "It would give you your life back."

For the first time in a long time, I felt relieved.

"Do you want to go ahead?" he asked.

"Yes." Julie and I both answered and nodded our heads at the same time. It sounded as if he was presenting a choice between alternatives, and we should carefully weigh up the pros and cons of each one. But I knew that there was really no choice. I had to move forward with the lung transplant option if I wanted to survive.

After the consultation, I was anxious to get on with the tests that would determine my suitability as a lung transplant candidate. No one seemed to be questioning any longer if I should have a lung transplant; it had moved to a question of when. I was feeling positive and confident that a lung transplant at this hospital was the right decision.

We had already met the lung transplant coordinator. Her role was to coordinate the next steps by scheduling the battery of medical tests. The coordinator is a patient's lifeline in preparing for evaluation and, ultimately, the lung transplant operation. She is the first point of contact, and coordinates all aspects, such as your records, your requests, your test appointments, the feedback on outcomes, and next steps. The lung transplant coordinator makes everything happen, and in many instances, your life is literally in her hands.

The coordinator is also the human face of an impersonal process. As a patient, you are going through a series of steps that are critical to your survival. The lung transplant coordinator recognizes the emotional rollercoaster ride that is an organ transplant for the patient and his or her family and helps to smooth out the worst of the bumps.

The tests had a dual purpose. They were designed to ascertain if a person was healthy enough, yet ill enough, to warrant an organ transplant. It was a strange position to be in, almost hoping to be sick enough to be given the chance of a new life with new lungs but hoping not to be so sick as to be disqualified from the procedure. There was a time window of opportunity for the operation and the patient had to be ready for that window. The tests were also designed to provide a medical map for the surgeons when they were performing the transplant surgery.

The testing was scheduled for the week after the Thanksgiving holiday and they were numerous and varied. One part of the assessment was a six-minute walk to help assess my lung functionality. For a marathon runner, it seemed laughable that I was going to be measured over such a trivial distance. At a brisk pace of four miles per hour, I should be able to walk 0.4 of a mile in six minutes. When I reported to the nurse, I half-expected to be taken outside to sprint around the parking lot.

Alas, no. Another complication was a recent diagnosis of pulmonary arterial hypertension (PAH). When the small arteries in the lungs narrowed, it was harder for blood to flow through them, which raised the pressure in my lungs. As my heart had to work harder because of the lung disease to pump blood through the arteries, it can easily lead to heart failure.

The nurse indicated that I was to be measured walking up and down one of the short corridors while towing my oxygen tank. I managed the first couple of laps without too much difficulty, but soon began to slow down as my coughing started. I felt more and more out of breath. It was one of these humbling moments when I had the realization that I was not as physically able as I thought.

"This is ludicrous," I thought to myself. "I can go much faster than this."

"How much longer?" I asked the nurse through panting breath, thinking that the six minutes must have been up quite a few minutes ago.

"Just over three minutes left," she said, looking at her watch. "Just go as far as you can."

I was still determined to break the hospital speed record for the six-minute-walk, so I pushed on and, after what seemed like an hour of walking - but it was only three more minutes - I finished the test, panting and coughing. I felt like I had just had a strenuous work-out and sucked in oxygen through my cannula.

"That will do for now," said the nurse, and she led me back to the waiting room.

We touched base with the transplant coordinator as the week of testing progressed. The tests were unpleasant, but I knew that they were necessary. I did not feel particularly well that week, and I had to tow my clanking oxygen tank wherever I went.

Even moving from test room to test room was exhausting. My constant concern was that the oxygen would run out, and I was always glancing surreptitiously at the tank's gauge to determine how long it would be before it needed to be replaced. Spare oxygen tanks were rolling around in the back of the car wherever we went and we had to carry extras whenever we went out or made the trip to the hospital. This only added to an already stressful situation.

I spoke to the transplant coordinator one day about some of the tests, and she made the comment that my CT scan looked "really good."

"What do you mean "really good?" I asked cautiously, hardly daring to believe that the scan had revealed a healthy picture of my lungs. I still nurtured a silent hope that this whole process was one big mistake and that any day now the doctors would concede that my lungs were just fine after all. But no, that wasn't happening today.

"By "really good," she said, a little embarrassed, "I mean that it looks good for getting you on the transplant list. Your lungs are in really bad shape."

By the end of the week, I was exhausted. I felt that it was only a matter of a few days before I was put on the list for my transplant. The average waiting time on the list was twelve to eighteen months, we were told. All I needed to do was to get onto the list. I mentally buried the earlier "six-months left" comment in the light of the waiting list timeframe.

I was asked to circle back to the specialist pulmonary clinic in Denver that I had consulted initially three years earlier. My lung condition fell into the broad category of interstitial lung disease and I was seen by one of the nation's foremost experts in this medical sub-specialty.

He must have been aware of my case and background as when I walked into his office, he commented, "You don't look as bad as I expected."

I was uncertain as to whether that was good or bad. He talked in general terms about lung transplant and commented that he had every reason to believe that I would have a successful transplant outcome. I was in "good hands," he said.

As I was leaving, he made a final comment. "The trouble with you," he said, looking at me pensively, "is that you are not a complainer."

I believe that he thought I was too stoical about my illness. I initially took this to be compliment, as I am engrained in the philosophy of "grin and bear it" in the face of adversity. Later, I thought it may have been a criticism. I suspect he was giving coded advice for me to self-advocate during the tough events he knew were ahead.

## Re-run

As a transplant novice, I underestimated the extent to which the array of tests could result in my being disqualified for the procedure. I believed that as I felt healthy and well – apart from my lungs – I would automatically be one of the strongest candidates for a transplant. It never crossed my mind that my medical condition would render me ineligible, at least in this hospital's opinion.

"Gavin, we need to run some of the tests again. Can you come in this week?" It was the transplant coordinator calling to tell me that I needed to come back to the clinic.

A week had passed since the conclusion of the first wave of testing and Julie and I were waiting anxiously for word from the hospital. To be recalled for additional testing was unexpected, to say the least.

"Everything's alright, isn't it?" I heard Julie asking when I passed the phone to her. "Yes," she was assured They just needed to "re-run some of the tests to get a more accurate picture of a few critical areas."

The next week – it was now the second week in December – I reluctantly reported back at the hospital for the additional tests. I was not particularly concerned by the recall. I just wanted the testing part to be over. Once the repeat tests were completed, another two weeks passed. We understood that my case was going to be put before the Transplant Committee any day. We were anxious to get confirmation.

We were at home. It was Friday, December 21st, 2007, four days before Christmas. The phone rang. It was the hospital. As soon as I answered the phone, I knew by the tone of the caller's voice that all was not well. "There is a problem," the doctor said. "It is unlikely that we will be able to do your transplant."

"What do you mean?" I gulped, scarcely able to comprehend.

"Well, there is a complicated pattern of collateral blood vessels around your lungs that have formed to compensate for the scale of your disease. It means your chest wall has many blood vessels that are not normally there. Our surgeons are concerned that there is a high risk that you will bleed to death on the operating table if we perform the surgery," he said. There was an awkward silence.

"Is there anything you can do?" I prompted. I couldn't think of what to ask. I couldn't believe what I was hearing.

"Well, we could go back and look at your case again, I suppose." He sounded reluctant. "I could discuss it again with the surgeons."

"Could you do that...please?" I could feel my voice fading off, as my stomach filled with dread.

"Okay, I will call you back on Wednesday," he said and rung off.

Essentially, we had to wait until Wednesday, December 26th - the day after Christmas - to hear back from the hospital. We waited with great trepidation as the days crawled by.

Zander and Riley were great as always. In fact, their positive attitude throughout the whole lung transplant ordeal was an important source of inspiration and strength. We had decided early on to be honest with them and tell them what was going on, but not to scare them. They were very nonchalant about the fact that their Dad spent most of the day lying on the couch or on his bed.

Riley, aged six, used to say "Hey, Dad, I can always find you in the house without calling for you. I just follow the tubes!" To her, the tubes served a useful purpose beyond providing oxygen. She often matter-of-factly mentioned to her friends at school that her "Daddy was waiting for a lung transplant," as if it was the most normal thing in the world.

Zander, aged eight, was quieter about the whole thing. He would not ask many questions, but he still enjoyed spending time with me, and would often lie up against me and read a book.

When Wednesday arrived, I couldn't wait for the doctor to call. I called him at 8:30 a.m., got his voice mail, and left a message for him to call me back. He eventually called back at 4:30 p.m. I silently passed the phone over to Julie.

She didn't say much during the short call. She nodded a lot, and I could tell a lot by her expression. She hung up.

"What did he say?"

"He gave me all sorts of reasons why they can't do the transplant," she said. "Apparently, they are now also concerned that your right diaphragm is paralyzed, and so even with new lungs you wouldn't be able to breathe." She looked at me and started to cry.

That was the end of our contact with the hospital. We did not receive any kind of official notification that I was not being considered for transplant any longer, nor any more specific reason for their denial. They just stopped communicating with us. The only reason I can speculate about for their refusal was their lack of surgical expertise to take on a challenging case. Whatever the reason, their response was opprobrious. I would have preferred a straight answer rather than just being cut adrift.

Quite apart from the shock of not being treated, we had wasted two full months of the six months of time that the doctors had predicted I had left.

Julie knew right away that we needed to find a new transplant center – and fast.

# CHAPTER FOUR: WE HAVE LUNGS FOR YOU

*"My head's under water*
*But I'm breathing fine*
*You're crazy and I'm out of my mind."*

- John Legend, *All of me*

## We need to find a new transplant center – and fast

I had not considered the possibility that I would be turned down by the hospital for transplant surgery. There was no contingency plan. I thought that we had reached the end of the road.

On the contrary, Julie's first thought was "where else can we go?" She immediately went online and began to search for other transplant centers. We knew we were under the gun as my lung disease was progressing. Three months before, I could walk, albeit slowly, without oxygen. Now I could barely lie still without oxygen.

The cannula that delivered supplementary oxygen through my nose would frequently slip out of place during the night. When that happened, I would wake up to the tortured feeling that I was being suffocated. My feet and legs would tingle from lack of oxygen. I would lunge over to grab the oxygen mask that was by my bed-side and turn the valve up to its maximum level. My breathing would normalize after several minutes of gasping and panting. It took much longer for the feelings of sheer panic to leave.

With the help of several personal contacts with pulmonary physicians and other medical specialists, Julie compiled a list of the top twenty-two transplant centers in the United States, which she evaluated for experience with complex fibrotic conditions.

Looking back, we probably should have prioritized the top five centers, but we knew that time was a precious commodity and that each center would take several days to evaluate my case and respond. We collected my medical records from the hospital records department and made twenty-two copies of all the paperwork, along with disks of the various x-rays and CT scans.

Julie made several requests to the doctor at the hospital to write a letter to summarize his medical findings to send to other potential transplant centers. Initially, he was reluctant to write the letter at all. Then, once he agreed, he said it would take him several days to complete. Julie told him that we did not have several days to waste and that she needed the letter post-haste. To her extreme frustration, the doctor continued to prevaricate. Her subsequent suggestion that she would chain herself to the railings at the hospital entrance with a bullhorn had the desired effect. The letter arrived the next day.

The letter spelled out a medical dystopia of a paralyzed diaphragm and impossibly misaligned blood vessels. It concluded that there was no hope for a successful lung transplant. We referred to that document as the "world's most depressing letter."

We had no choice but to shrug off this setback and focus on the task at hand. Within a few days, we had couriered out twenty-two individual packages of medical information to the transplant centers we had identified.

From her work as a medical communications specialist, Julie was also on first name terms with several leading pulmonologists in different parts of the United States. She did not hesitate to call them up and ask for their opinions. "If it was your family member, where would you go for a lung transplant?" she asked.

At least seventeen of the transplant centers we contacted either sent us a letter that stated they would not accept me as a patient or told us by phone that I would not be accepted. The rejection determinations were made after a seemingly cursory review of my medical information, including the ominous letter, or simply because I had been turned down by the first hospital. I felt dejected and angry.

Despite the deluge of rejections, three transplant centers looked as if they would offer an evaluation: University of Pittsburgh Medical Center, Cleveland Clinic and Duke University Medical Center. We discovered quickly that the University of Pittsburgh would not accept my brand of health care insurance, so the short list quickly became even shorter: the Cleveland Clinic in Ohio or Duke University Medical Center (hereafter "Duke") in North Carolina.

We were in contact with other institutions that had responded to the FedEx packages. In our hastily arranged telephone "interviews," several centers touted the strength of the medical credentials of their transplant programs because "our surgeons were trained at Duke."

After you hear that for the third or fourth time, you start thinking "why don't I go to Duke?" The lung transplant coordinator at Duke said that the average waiting time on the list at Duke was only twenty-one days. This short time seemed incredible, especially when I had been quoted an average waiting time of twelve to eighteen months in Colorado. It did not take long for Duke's reputation and its average organ waiting time to clinch the deal for me.

There was a direct flight from Denver to Raleigh-Durham, and I saw on the internet that the temperature in North Carolina in February was in the seventies[4]. I made up my mind.

"Let's go to Duke," I said to Julie.

Julie called them back and arranged for an appointment. I was discouraged to hear that Duke was going to make me go through the entire series of tests again despite having all my medical records. Time would show that Duke was entirely right in re-running the tests although, at that moment, I felt like they were unnecessarily repeating work that had already been done, and so wasting precious time.

We got the appointment for the second week in February 2008.

## Onward

The flight to Raleigh-Durham was complicated by the fact that I had to travel with supplementary oxygen. We had to arrange to leave the portable oxygen tanks at the boarding gate at the airport, walk onto the aircraft without oxygen - easier said than done - then use the on-board oxygen during the flight. On

---

4    24°C

arrival at Raleigh-Durham airport, I had to disembark without oxygen, then picked up pre-arranged portable oxygen bottles at the arrival gate.

A slow week followed. We made sure we were on time for every appointment and every interview. We met my designated transplant pulmonologist and the lung transplant coordinator. The staff at Duke was helpful in getting me from appointment to appointment, while I dealt with moving around with supplementary oxygen. At this point, I could barely walk, even with the assistance of the oxygen, so I had to be pushed around in a wheel chair.

It soon became clear why Duke was redoing many of the tests. Duke's physicians only had confidence in testing that was done by their own team at their own location, which worked in my favor.

"We don't see a lot of the complications that were highlighted by the hospital in Colorado," one pulmonologist said. "I expect you will be transplanted within three weeks."

I was astounded that he was so confident. It seemed that the physicians at Duke took a certain pride in taking on difficult or complicated surgical cases that other hospitals had turned down.

However, even though I was pleased and relieved, it also made me a little nervous that we were moving briskly towards the transplant itself. In our rush to overcome the obstacles of being rejected for treatment, I had almost forgotten what was ahead. I knew in my heart that it was essential for me to get the operation but, at the same time, I was nervous at the thought of having my lungs removed.

### Hour-glass therapeutics

During one of the tests, Julie had a side conversation with one of the pulmonologists. She broached the topic of how much time was left. This was a topic I had always avoided as I didn't want to hear someone's opinion – even an informed opinion – about how long it was before I died. There always seemed to be an element of self-fulfilling prophecy in these types of predictions.

In my opinion, if you are convinced that you are going to die, then you probably will.

One hospital's website noted that a lung transplant would not be considered until the patient had less than two years to live. I also knew that lung transplant – like any organ transplant – was a medical therapy of last resort. I knew I had end-stage lung disease and was in the "end of life" category, but I still didn't really believe it, despite everything I had been through.

"He can probably go until June without a lung transplant, but not much longer," Julie was told. It was February so that meant four months. Julie didn't tell me that piece of information until after my transplant, but she knew that we did not have a lot of time. Nevertheless, although I didn't know the exact time frame, I was acutely aware how I felt. And I felt that my lung functionality was rapidly deteriorating.

At the early stages of my lung disease, I did not notice how much weight I was losing or my impaired lung function, as the deterioration was so gradual. Now, in February 2008, I could tell I was deteriorating more rapidly than before. Even the shortest of walks would send me into a spasm of coughing which, in turn, sent my oxygen saturation level plummeting. That left me more susceptible to a heart attack, due to the increased workload on my cardiovascular system. I had to move around as little as possible, with a task as simple as brushing my teeth requiring rest breaks.

Around that time, Julie and I were going through some required paperwork with a nurse. "You need to consider this one carefully," the nurse said. I wasn't sure what she meant.

"Do you agree to accept high-risk organs?" she asked, reading from a form.

"What do you mean by "high-risk," I asked cautiously.

"Lungs that might come from a person with a high-risk profile. It could be a prostitute, a drug user, a felon. You know, high-risk."

No, I didn't know. I hadn't thought about it. I wasn't sure what to do. I looked at Julie. She shrugged back at me.

44

"I don't know," I said. "What do you think I should do?"

"I can't officially make a recommendation," she replied, somewhat defensively. She paused, then looked round conspiratorially at the door as if to confirm it was closed tightly.

"But if I were you," she said slowly, "I would take what comes up. You are in no position to be choosy."

She was right. It would be difficult enough to be matched with a good pair of lungs at the right time. So many things could go wrong with identifying organs, transporting them to the hospital, putting them in, and recovering. I could ill afford to limit the already small pool of availability any further by eliminating any potential organs.

"Yes, I'll accept whatever comes up," I confirmed. Julie was nodding in agreement. I reached forward and scribbled my signature on the consent form.

## Listed

By the following Tuesday, I got a phone call from Duke.

"You'll be on the list by tomorrow, latest Thursday," she informed me. We just need to fill out some UNOS[5] paperwork and you're there. Congratulations!"

I felt like crying with relief. We had done it; I had made the lung transplant list.

Now I was listed, the next stop was a meeting with the transplant surgeon. This surgeon had the reputation of being brilliant but with a rather brusque manner. Julie and I had an appointment to see him one afternoon at his office at the clinic. As he entered the windowless room and shook hands, I could see that he was not one for humor. His first words were "I'm going to scare you."

And scare us he did. He started with a fifteen-minute diatribe about everything that could go wrong with the operation including, but not limited to, the fact that the operation might

---

5    United Network for Organ Sharing (UNOS) is the private, non-profit organization that manages the United States' organ transplant system under contract with the federal government

take up to twelve hours, I might be in hospital for up to four months afterwards, and there was a chance I might bleed to death during the procedure.

I was aware during the extensive work up prior to being placed on the waiting list that my lungs had developed in an unusual way due to the lung disease. My body had "grown" extra blood vessels in the chest cavity to allow my body to get as much oxygen as possible. The extra blood vessels had attached themselves to my chest wall. Consequently, the operation to remove the lungs would involve cutting away these additional blood vessels and sealing them before the old lungs were removed. The process of severing the blood vessels would involve the risk of excessive bleeding.

With hindsight, I should have been ecstatic that the discussion with the surgeon focused on the problems of the surgery, as opposed to if it could be done at all. He knew that I had been turned down by the hospital in Colorado. He was not too interested in why I had been turned down, only that I presented a challenging case. The closest he got to smiling was when he commented that his team at Duke often got the difficult cases that other transplant centers would not accept.

He wound up the meeting by asking us how long we had been married. I replied that it was almost ten years. "Well, that's good," he said dryly. "It will take all your resilience to get through this."

Julie and I left the meeting with the surgeon in a daze. From our research, we knew the risks associated with lung transplant, and that my transplant was going to be riskier than most due to the blood vessel complication. I felt convinced that the fact that I was only forty-one years old and had been in excellent physical health must count heavily in my favor. I felt a simultaneous rush of relief and despair. So much to think about. So many unknowns. So much stress. I burst into tears.

### Dry runs

Another thing that I had not anticipated was dry runs. A dry run is a fire drill. You are told that a matching set of lungs is available and that you need to report to hospital immediately but, for some reason, the lungs are deemed unacceptable for transplant, and the operation does not go ahead. I had three dry runs before the real thing.

The first call came within twenty-four hours of being on the list. It was just after midnight when my bedside cell phone rang the first time. I grabbed the phone.

"Gavin? It's Katrina from lung transplant. Good news. We have a match. Nothing to eat or drink. You can come in through the emergency room."

This was it. It was really happening. Julie and I jumped out of bed. I felt a rush of excitement and nervousness at the same time. It took us less than five minutes to get dressed and dash out to the car, oxygen tank in tow. Julie drove quickly along the deserted highway and we got to the hospital in less than twenty minutes. On the way, we called our families to alert them to what was happening.

We entered the hospital through the emergency room and, once the receptionist had established why I was there, we were quickly escorted to the pulmonology unit on the seventh floor. The nurses kicked into a well-oiled routine as soon as I arrived. Before long, I had showered with anti-bacterial soap, changed into a hospital gown, and had an intravenous site set up in my arm.

People began coming in with a stream of consent forms. They were very clear about all the things that could go wrong during the operation: potential complications, risks of permanent disability, and death. None of it phased me at this point. I scribbled my signature on all the forms without hesitation or questions.

The anesthesiologist came in to reassure me that they would do everything they could to ensure a successful outcome. His friendly and relaxed demeanor gave me some much-needed confidence.

Then we had to wait. No one could tell us how long we would wait. It depended on several factors. The first one was the distance from which the organs were coming. Duke had its own helicopter that took off and landed on the hospital roof. As the nurse informed us, when a person was declared brain-dead and the family had given the consent to him or her being an organ donor, a match for the organs was quickly established based on blood type and physical size of the organs. Once that was done, the various hospitals were contacted to prepare for the transplants.

At that point, the organs had not been examined by surgeons to determine their transplant viability. This would generally only be done once the organs were recovered from the donor's body. Usually, the lungs are the last organs to be removed. Once the surgeons made an initial assessment, the lungs were recovered and transported in an iced cooler as quickly as possible to the recipient's hospital.

I had to wait until the organs arrived. The lungs would be inspected and approved by a surgeon who traveled in the helicopter and they were re-examined by another surgeon at the recipient hospital. If they were declared to be in good enough condition, I would be transferred to the pre-operation ("pre-op") area. The atmosphere was very tense.

We had waited for four hours in the pulmonology unit when the phone rang. It was the lung transplant coordinator, Katrina, who told us that the lungs were no good. I could go home again. It is difficult to describe the emotional anticlimax when I heard the news. It was like the sudden deflation of a vast balloon ready for take-off. However, as Julie pointed out, I would rather wait and get a pair of lungs that was in the best shape possible. We had waited this long. We could wait a few more days.

In the three weeks while I was on the list, I participated in the pre-operative program at the Duke Center for Living. Exercising at the Center for Living, even in my impaired state, certainly helped me make it through the difficult and emotionally draining waiting period.

Although I was on oxygen, I could make my way around the three-hundred-meter indoor track under my own steam, albeit with the wheeled oxygen tank dragging behind me. If I ran low on oxygen, I only had to signal to one of the respiratory therapists, and they would come over and change my tank. In this way, I could exercise as much as possible to ready myself for the trauma of the imminent transplant surgery.

Other patients who had already had their surgery were a good source of information for those of us who were waiting. For the first few days, the newly transplanted patients were a little spaced out due to the drugs they were on, but they quickly became more coherent. I asked all kinds of questions: how long were you in the ICU, how quickly did you walk, was it painful, what was the worst part? All the information helped the rest of us mentally prepare for what was to come.

There were two more dry run calls over the next two weeks. Both times, we reported to the hospital promptly and went through the surgical preparation, only to be informed that the lungs were unacceptable. The second dry run lasted for over twenty hours while we waited in the hospital. That was experience was both physically and mentally exhausting for all of us.

Then came the fourth call, twenty-two days after I was put on the list. My phone rang at 6:30 p.m. on Thursday evening as I was lying on my bed in the hotel room, breathing oxygen from the omnipresent tube.

"Gavin? It's Cindy from lung transplant. Good news. We have lungs for you. Nothing to eat or drink. Come to the main reception at the hospital."

After three dry runs, I was sure that it was going to happen this time. Julie put her foot down and we reached the hospital in record time. If we had been stopped by a traffic cop, we would have had an awesome excuse for speeding. We parked the car and scrambled to the hospital reception to check in.

I felt elated and nervous at the same time; elated because I believed that my chance to receive the gift of a new set of lungs that would save my life had arrived, and nervous about the surgery that I was going to go through. Even though butterflies churned through my stomach, I was determined to go ahead.

49

Three hours later, I was lying in a bed in the pulmonary unit, showered, blood checked, and intravenous needle in my arm. I must have dozed off when the phone rang. It was 2:00 a.m.

## The lungs are good

"Gavin, everything is fine. The lungs are good. We are ready to go," said the reassuring voice. I was beyond caring who was speaking. I sank back and let out a sigh of relief. This was it. We were ready to go. I kissed Julie as two nurses wheeled me out of the pulmonology ward and into the pre-op area.

After so much waiting, everything seemed to move very quickly. There was intense activity all around, as the nurses and doctors prepared for surgery. I remember noticing how warm the whole room felt as I lay there. I didn't have my glasses, so the nurses and doctors around me were out of focus. The intravenous needle in my arm was connected to a sedative, which flowed steadily into my veins.

I was glad it was all moving forward. At the same time, I was anxious about feeling so out of control. I had to leave everything in the hands of the experts. I visualized that I was going to wake up in what would seem like mere minutes with perfect new lungs.

Everyone was now moving around me in a strange slow motion. I could make out noise, but could not make out what people were saying any longer. Sounds blended together. The blanket was so warm and comfortable. I closed my eyes as the anesthetic did its work. Darkness enveloped me as I slipped into unconsciousness.

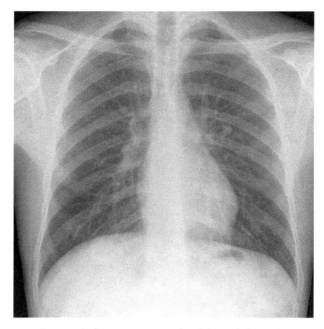

Normal chest x-ray in a healthy adult male

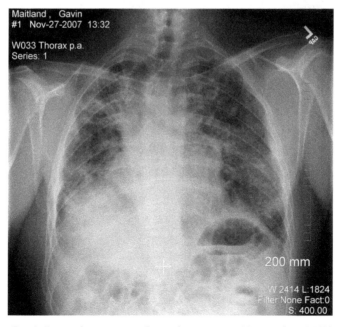

Gavin's pre-lung transplant chest x-ray. November 2007

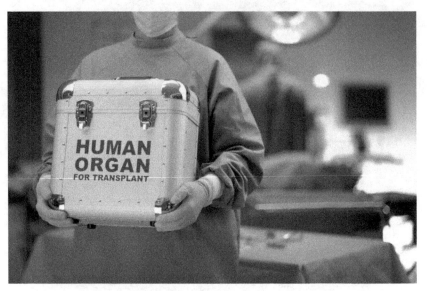

Transporting an organ for transplant

# CHAPTER FIVE: BOSTON HARBOR SWIM

*Swimming is not a sport. Swimming is a way to keep from drowning. That's just common sense.*

- George Carlin

## Six years post-transplant: raising awareness

It is fascinating to see an elite athlete up close, and even more so if you are competing against him.

My daughter Riley and I were sitting across from Alex Meyer, the United States Olympic open-water swimmer on the first of four water taxis in the inner Boston harbor at 8:00 a.m. on Saturday, September 20th, 2014. The water taxis were transporting over three hundred swimmers on the one-mile journey across Boston harbor from Moakley Courthouse at Fan Pier in South Boston to the swim start at Piers Park Sailing Center in east Boston.

It is always exciting to be in Boston. The harbor occupies such an important place in American history. Discovered to Europeans in 1614 by the British adventurer, John Smith, it is the site of the famous Tea Party, as well as being the focal point of nearly all imports to the New England coastal areas through to the nineteenth century.

Alex Meyers placed tenth in the 2012 Olympics Games in the ten-kilometer open-water swim event, and his credits include winning the Open Water World Championships over 15.6 miles[6] in 2010. This morning, he did not look particularly Olympian. He sat slumped in a seat, the hood of his swim jacket pulled over his head, eating muffins from a paper bag.

The lower deck of the water taxi was enclosed and warm. I was glad. One of my concerns had been getting cold prior to entering the water. Riley and I spoke to one our fellow competitors as the boat moved away from the dock.

"Have you done the swim before?" the man next to us asked.

---

6    25 km

"No, first time."

"Same for me," he said. "How old are you?" he asked, looking at Riley.

"Thirteen," she replied brightly.

The man raised his eyebrows. "Good luck!"

The swim this morning was organized by Enviro-Sport, a California-based group under the banner of Sharkfest Swims. They organize swim events across the country, mostly one to two miles in length.

"Could they not have picked a better name?" my mother-in-law commented nervously when she heard about the swim. She was undoubtedly considering the sanity of allowing her beloved granddaughter to fend off a predator.

"It's fine. Sharkfest is just a name," I reassured her breezily. "There are no sharks in Boston harbor." At least, that's what it says on the website, I thought to myself. She did not say anymore but continued to eye the event's jaws-like logo with suspicion.

"We have three hundred and twenty-two swimmers this morning, so we're going in four waves of eighty," yelled the large man in a bright red sweatshirt once we were on the other side of the harbor. He continued with the pre-swim briefing as we all bunched towards him. His stentorian roar boomed out with little need for a megaphone.

"Go in the first wave if you are aiming to place in your age group. Go in the last wave if you want to be at the back. Everyone else goes in between. Jump in and start swimming at the sound of the horn!"

I estimated that about a quarter of the swimmers were not wearing wetsuits. Apart from keeping cold at bay, a wetsuit provides additional buoyancy and the lets you swim a little faster due to less drag. However, among experienced open-water swimmers, there is a certain cachet about swimming without a wetsuit. The water temperature was officially declared at sixty-two degrees[7], so the cold was not prohibitive. Riley and I were both wearing wetsuits that sunny autumn morning.

---

7    About 17°C

As the horn sounded, waves one, two and three of swimmers jumped off the wooden dock. The water turned white with turbulence as arms thrashed and legs kicked. Riley and I were in the fourth wave. As the horn went off and I jumped, I was surprised how cool and soft the water felt. Rising to the surface, I started breast stroking until I could disentangle myself from the mayhem of swimming neighbors. I caught my breath as I made some space and eased into freestyle.

My eyes scanned ahead, looking alternately for a glimpse of Riley, the mass of swimmers, and the city's skyline. I caught glimpses above the surface as I raised my head between strokes. All I could see was a morass of swim caps and splashing. It was impossible to distinguish an individual swimmer, so I gave up, put my head down and focused on swimming across the harbor.

**Early days**

The start of the modern age of open-water swimming is often believed to be Lord Byron's classic swim across the Dardanelles in 1810, a narrow strait in north-west Turkey, formerly known as the Hellespont. The English poet was the first swimmer to make the crossing in modern times, in honour of the Greek mythological figure, Leander. It looks like a great swim, only three miles from the continent of Asia to the continent of Europe. When the modern Olympic Games began in 1896, the short distance swimming competitions were of course in open-water. The 2008 Games in Beijing were the first to include a ten-kilometer open-water race, followed by the 2012 London Games and the 2016 Rio de Janeiro Games, reflecting the sport's growing popularity.

To many people, long-distance swimming means a challenge like crossing the English Channel, often considered by to be one of the toughest swims. To make a crossing officially recognized by the rule-setting body, the English Channel Swimming Association, only a swim suit, cap, and goggles are allowed – and definitely no wetsuits.

Three times as many people have conquered Mount Everest

than have successfully swum the English Channel. Measuring twenty-one miles as the crow flies, swimmers typically swim at least thirty miles due to the currents when making the England-to-France crossing.

I am always interested in swims that push out barriers. In August 2014, a seventy-year-old Australian became the oldest person to swim the English Channel. One month later, the record was broken again by Otto Thaning, a seventy-three-year-old South African heart surgeon. In a radio interview, he articulated how he felt.

"When I eventually stepped clear of the water... I was absolutely exhilarated to the point of tears. It was wonderful," he said.

There is undoubtedly something unique about a sport that can lead an older athlete to describe such a monumental physical and mental feat as emotional and "wonderful."

Terry Laughlin, a swim coach, recounted why he swam across the Gibraltar Strait in 2013. He swam with two friends and they synchronized their strokes for the entire nine-mile[8] crossing from Spain to Morocco. "It takes enormous concentration to keep in synch with two other swimmers for such a long time," he commented. "That degree of focus has always been a great source of pleasure for me."

In both cases, I understood exactly what they meant.

## Early morning elation

The morning sunshine pierced directly into my eyes as I turned my head to breathe. One of the motorized support boats on my left was a little too close for comfort. I could smell the diesel fumes across the water. I turned to my right side to breathe for the next and following inhalations.

The Boston city skyline was much closer now. Riley was somewhere, but I couldn't see her anywhere in the forest of swimmers and kayaks. The early morning swell of the harbor had subsided and the water was smooth. I felt pleased that my

---

8    14km

stroke was consistent, and my breathing was calm and rhythmic. Coming in from Boulder, Colorado, at 5,430 feet[9], I could fully appreciate the sensation of additional available oxygen in the Boston sea-level air. And I always smile when I think of the marketing slogan of the *Bolder Boulder* ten-kilometer run, held every year on Memorial Day: *Sea Level is for Sissies.*

I have often wanted to figure out what benefit, if any, I got from swimming at sea-level compared to Boulder, so I consulted San Diego-based coach and personal trainer, Marika Page. Marika has lived and trained at the nine thousand, six hundred feet[10] elevation of Breckenridge, Colorado. She is also a former US national lightweight rower, so she is a bit of a strenuous cardiovascular exercise guru.

"If you tend to be more of a slow twitch athlete, you will get less benefit from going to sea level," she said, referring to muscle fibers more common among endurance athletes. Sprinters usually have a higher blend of fast twitch fibers. The fiber of most people's muscles lies somewhere in the middle of fast and slow.

"The more you are fifty-fifty fast twitch-slow twitch, the bigger the improvement when you go to sea level," she continued. "But," she cautioned, "anyone who says they can quantitively tell you what your improvement is going to be at sea level is full of bunk. It's super individual."

Will I get any physiological benefit at all at sea level, I ask, somewhat disappointedly? "Can I guarantee you're going to get faster? Probably not. However, you will likely be able to maintain your race pace for a longer time. In a distance event, your time will likely improve, as you feel more comfortable for longer at your race pace than you did at altitude. Mentally, that helps a lot," she said.

Given my affinity for endurance events, I would guess that I am firmly in the slow twitch camp. It's no magic swimming bullet, but perhaps the psychological benefit of knowing there is more available oxygen in the sea-level air has some positive

9    1,655m
10   2,926m

subliminal effect. I'll take it, I thought, as I savored every oxygenated inhalation.

There is a huge sense of accomplishment from completing a physical challenge, coupled with open-water. There is something awe-inspiring, humbling, and even mystical about it. Space is seemingly limitless on all sides – above, below, all around you. As humans, we have an undeniable affinity for water - over seventy percent of the surface of our home, the Earth, is blue and our very bodies are made up of sixty percent water – even though evolution has left us poorly designed for swimming.

Just as Zen Buddhism emphasizes the use of meditation and intuition, so open-water swimming can provide its own source of serenity and magic. For many athletes, it fills the mental space normally filled by the problems and distractions of day-to-day life.

As a swimmer, resistance is your adversary. You need to displace the same amount of water as your body mass, no easy task as water is eight hundred times denser than air. However – and this is the important part – your apparent enemy, the water, also supports you and propels you forward. Your very enemy becomes your friend.

Many would agree that this is analogous to life itself. The problems we often encounter in life can also support us and make us stronger in the process. Personally, I invariably use these life lessons to overcome the inevitable medical challenges and complexities of lung transplant. I have developed an unusual appreciation for overcoming adversity. Swimming has been a constant source of physical and spiritual nourishment during my recovery although my family still finds lung-transplant and open-water swimming something of a hair-raising combination.

As a perpetual patient (the words "a lung transplant is not a cure, it simply exchanges one set of health problems for another" often echo in my mind), I try to prevent my transplant from defining my life. Swimming affords me this luxury. It allows me to compete on the same level playing field as everyone else.

A kayaker hovered nearby, as I was swimming close the back of the group. If I paused my stroke and let my body hang in the water - what swim safety crews refer to as an "upright" - she would check in that I was doing well.

"Yes, fine," I replied. "Just enjoying the view." In these brief pauses, I could see the sunlit panorama of high-rise buildings of the Boston waterfront. From the middle of the harbor, I was enjoying sunlight and city views which escape most visitors.

The water felt clean although, as a single-minded swimmer, it would have to be really dirty before I would notice. People familiar with Boston often raised their eyebrows at the idea of swimming across the harbor due to the perceived pollution. After the swim, I mentioned the swim to my dental hygienist, John Nathan, a Boston-native. He paused in mid-tooth scrape and said with incredulity, "You *swam* in Boston harbor?" But this morning, the water seemed wonderfully clean and gloriously salty.

In a snap, the finish was in sight. I reached the harbor wall and hauled myself up the quayside ladder. The team of finishers recorded my entry number – inked on the back of my hand – and I looked around for Riley.

I felt elated, yet mildly disappointed. Elated because I had covered the one mile in just over thirty minutes and disappointed because the swim was over so quickly. If someone had said I had to turn around and swim back to the start, I would have gladly done so.

I found Riley in the melee of finishers, which allowed me to take a breath of relief. She had finished several minutes in front of me, as I knew she would, and had swum across the harbor as if it was a Sunday stroll, which I also knew she would. Nevertheless, I felt relieved when I found her. We sat down together on a patch of warm grass to relax and catch up.

In addition to swimming for fun, the swim was a novel way for Riley and me to contribute to raising awareness of organ donation. If people asked about it, we would say, "Yes, we swam Boston harbor. Be an organ, eye, and tissue donor!"

The Olympian, Alex Meyer, took first place with a swim of just over sixteen minutes – yes, sixteen minutes! He wore only a swim suit, swim cap, goggles, and a small portable camera strapped to his forehead. Riley was second in her age-group, 75th overall. I was 22nd in my age-group, 155th overall.

"Dad, the Olympic swimmer swam twice as fast as you," Riley chirped as we walked from the finish area after the awards ceremony. She was studying the printout of the posted race results. It was hard to escape her perspicacity.

Well, yes." I reflected for a moment. I could point out that he was in his mid-twenties, compared to my late forties, and I doubted if he had undergone a double-lung transplant. But I settled with, "I think he probably does more training than I do. Maybe I should step up the pace. What do you think?"

Yes," she replied, nodding pensively. "You probably should."

## Lost in translation

Some months later, I was talking to a young man about swimming. He had previously completed the Alcatraz swim, and we were swapping cold-water stories. I told him about Boston.

He nodded his head in appreciation at my description of the swim across the harbor.

"Boston harbor, that's gnarly," he grinned.

Gnarly? I did not understand. There is a tongue-in-cheek saying about how Britain and the United States are two countries separated by a common language. Having lived among the locals for several years now, I thought that I had a fair degree of fluency in the American English. I regularly take out the trash instead of the rubbish, and confidently walk on sidewalks instead of pavements, although my family reminds me that I routinely mispronounce - at least to their ears - words like vitamins, tomatoes and garage. Reminding them who came up with the language in the first place gets me nowhere. But this one had me totally flummoxed. Gnarly?

"Thanks!", I said, somewhat baffled. It was all I could think of. Boston harbor has long had a reputation for being polluted, but the swim itself had been a wonderful experience. The Urban Dictionary told me that gnarly means, depending on the context, one of three things: either bumpy or twisted, difficult or very bad, or very good. I was none the wiser.

Even after thinking about it, I still don't really know what he meant. Perhaps that harbor water was dirty, that the swim was challenging, or that the swim was easy. Regardless of what he meant, I take it as compliment and am proud that Riley and I swam across Boston harbor that day.

# CHAPTER SIX: ROAD TO RECOVERY

*"It's great to be here. It's great to be anywhere."*
　　　　- Keith Richards, *guitarist*, The Rolling Stones

## Pulling up from a nose-dive

Wow, I can breathe! As soon as I awoke, despite my anesthesia-induced drowsiness, I realized I couldn't see, couldn't speak, and couldn't move. But I could breathe. I took another tentative breath. Then another. I could feel my diaphragm expanding as my chest filled with exquisite air. Lying in the darkness, I smiled to myself.

I hadn't experienced clear breaths for a long time. The deterioration of my lungs over the past six years meant that my breathing had steadily become more restricted. Each breath was short and shallow, as my lung functionality shrank to a meagre thirty percent of normal. I took another deep breath, relishing in the depth to which I could expand my chest.

I was aware of people in the room. I knew my hands were tethered to the bedside to prevent me from involuntarily pulling out the breathing tube. I didn't know why I couldn't see, but I couldn't open my eyes. I was aware that my wife, Julie, was standing next to the bed, saying something. I strained but couldn't make out the words.

I flexed the fingers on my right hand. They felt stiff and unresponsive. I opened and closed my hand several times. I could hear the voice in my head. *"You must get up and walk!"* I forced all my energy into my index and middle fingers.

*"Walk,"* they had said. *"It is vitally important that you walk as soon as possible after your operation. You must use your new lungs."*

My fingers felt stiff, but I pushed them to wiggle into what I thought was a walking motion.

"What's he doing?" I heard Julie say. "Why is he doing that?"

She thought I was having a spasm. I could tell she didn't understand. I couldn't make a sound, so I made a hand gesture of holding a pen. I heard Julie reacting. "A pen, get a pen, he wants to write!"

A second later, I felt a pen in my hand and started to scrawl the word W-A-L-K on the paper.

"He wants to walk!" I heard Julie say. Jubilant, relieved.

Afterwards, Julie told me how comical it was. I was lying in the intensive care unit at Duke Hospital. There seemed to be a million tubes coming out of me connected to all kinds of boxes, drips, and electronic equipment, a two-foot-long scar across my chest, and a respirator tube down my throat. I had just survived a five-and-a half hour operation that had replaced both lungs. When Julie said, "He wants to walk!" the nurse looked at her humorlessly and said, "I don't think so."

I was confused for the next few hours as I lapsed in and out of consciousness. The respirator was withdrawn, and my hands were released. I was so hot. I asked the nurse to give me bags of ice cubes, which I put under my feet. The tightness of my skin made me squirm with discomfort. I started shivering. I was so cold.

The effects of the drugs over the past few hours, as well as the effects of the anesthetic, made me feel unsettled. I was experiencing the effects of massive doses of prednisone, the anti-inflammatory and immuno-suppressive drug, that acted to prevent my body from rejecting the transplanted organs. I felt like climbing the walls. In the weeks leading up to the transplant operation, I had been on a daily prednisone dose of five milligrams. During the operation, the dosage had been jacked up to five hundred milligrams.

## Bronch

The best way pulmonologists can get a window into the new lungs was via a bronchoscopy. A three-foot tube with a tiny camera on the end was inserted through the nostrils and pushed into the lungs for a visual examination and to take a tissue sample. I wasn't going to be given much of a break. Hours after waking up from the surgery, I endured the first of several rounds of bronchoscopies.

It would usually go like this: a doctor would assure me that it would be just a little uncomfortable. I would put my head back and try to breathe through my mouth. The tube would go down through my nose without sedation and I would feel like I was drowning. Fortunately, the ordeal didn't last more than a few minutes before the tube was withdrawn. I had usually stopped gasping and my eyes stopped watering after thirty minutes.

I knew from briefings that I would be kept "dry" after the transplant, as the doctors believed that the lungs would settle in better without fluid. In practice, that meant I would get nutrition through an intravenous drip for now, and a feeding tube later, for several weeks. I wasn't allowed to drink anything, not even a sip of water. It was the driest that I had ever felt. My mouth was constantly parched.

I had longer periods of consciousness. I tried to focus my eyes on the nurse who was monitoring the dials and lights. A large bottle of mineral water was sitting on her desk. It tortured me as I watched her pick it up and take a long drink.

"Could you get rid of that bottle of water, please?" I croaked. She looked surprised, but nonetheless took the bottle out of the room. I fell back to sleep.

I woke up as a couple of nurses pushed an x-ray film onto the illuminated screen on the wall of the room. They didn't seem to be aware that I was partially-awake.

"His lungs are in great shape," one of them said, looking at the film.

I couldn't help but overhear them. I felt relieved that the lungs were fabulous, although uncomfortable that they were reading the x-ray in front of me. What if the lungs weren't in good condition? Would they have said, "His lungs are in terrible shape!" Happily, that wasn't the case. I drifted back to sleep.

It wasn't until evening that I started to feel more coherent again. The idea of walking didn't seem so crazy anymore. I asked the nurse again if it was time to walk. She said not yet, but maybe soon.

About midnight on Friday night, eighteen hours after receiving my new lungs, a man in sweats bounced into my room. He looked like he had just come from playing tennis. He introduced himself as the physical therapist. He was going to help get me up.

"How do you feel?" he grinned. "Ready to walk?"

"Sure," I replied. "But what about all this stuff?" I gestured at the drainage tubes coming from my body, as well as the drip, the blood pressure cuff, and the epidural wire in my back.

"We'll take it all with us!" he replied cheerfully. He deftly piled up the boxes and connectors and stacked them on two wheeled stands, and proudly announced "Okay, ready!"

I gingerly swung my legs out of bed, mindful of the catheter. The therapist helped me to put on some slippers. I stood up slowly. The therapist was standing over me in case I keeled over, but I waved him away. "I feel fine," I lied. "Let's go!"

He pushed a walker over to me, and I grasped the handles. I shuffled out of the intensive care unit and out into the corridor, feeling like I was the hundred-year-old man[11]. I moved along, passing other recovering transplant patients in various states of consciousness in glass-fronted rooms. Together, we walked down the corridor at a snail's pace, balancing the accessories on the stands. We got to the end of the corridor, turned around, and started back to my room. "Feel good?" he asked.

"Feel fine," I replied.

And I did feel fine. I could walk and breathe on my own. I no longer needed the accursed supplementary oxygen tank. I felt like punching the air with elation.

We got back to my room, and I climbed back into bed. My legs were shaking from the exertion and the effect of the drugs.

"Well done," said the therapist. "You'll do just fine." He was beaming broadly.

A couple of hours later, around 2:00 a.m. on Saturday morning, a nurse came into my room. "We think you are ready to go to the stepdown unit," she said.

---

11  Oblique reference to the dark-humored novel "The 100-Year-Old Man Who Climbed Out the Window and Disappeared" by Jonas Jonasson (2012)

"Okay," I replied. I knew that patients weren't discharged from the intensive care unit until they were ready, so was pleased to have cleared this hurdle.

"Do you want to walk there?" the nurse asked. "It's not very far. A hundred yards or so."

"Yes, I'll try," I said. The nurse called a colleague, and together they loaded the drainage boxes, the drips, and other accessories onto the stands, and helped me out of bed again. I walked as upright as I could, with as much dignity as I could muster in the open-backed hospital gown. As I passed the nurses' station at the entrance to the stepdown unit, there were three or four nurses there. The nurse with me said, "Look at this! He's walking less than twenty-four hours after lung transplant!"

The nurses at the station all stood up and started applauding. That is the only standing ovation I have ever received. I managed a smile and a half-wave. As I reached my room, it seemed as if I had just overcome an obstacle of Himalayan dimensions. I was uncomfortable, tired, and woozy, but also reassured that I had passed the first physical test. I took a deep breath. I was psychologically ready for the next one.

I settled into my room on the eighth floor at Duke Hospital and contemplated my situation. It was March 2008, and I had just had a double-lung transplant. It was the first time that it really hit home that I had someone else's lungs in my chest. It was the first of many times that I thought about the donor and his or her family. I could scarcely imagine the pain and suffering they must have gone through just a few hours earlier.

I needed to be stable enough to go home, but also needed to be able to cope without the medical team's support. As one of the nurses said, my goal was to get rid of as many of the tubes and support equipment as soon as possible.

My pre-operative canvassing of various post-transplant recipients at the rehabilitation center made me think a stay in hospital of about ten days was likely. I counted eight tubes that were coming out of my chest and side. Most were drainage tubes, where dark fluid flowed into bed-side transparent plastic measurement boxes. An epidural wire came from my back and extended into a primitive looking box that slowly dispensed a pain-killing drug. Every thirty minutes or so, I would blow into a box-like device that measured my breathing volume. I still had some way to go before I hit the target markings.

The incision on my chest was covered with a single strip of tape. I could feel the crude-looking staples that kept the incision together. The scar itself was two feet long from armpit to armpit in a clam-like shape across my chest. I would frequently cough up mucus from the depths of my new lungs, so the nurses had provided a red heart-shaped cushion to press against the chest incision during these coughing episodes.

No one actually said as much, but it must be designed to prevent the chest from bursting open during a coughing fit, I thought dramatically. I was propped up in the bed in a sitting position. Although it was the best position during the day, upright night-time sleeping was not so straight forward.

## One day at a time

Days were filled by doctors and nurses coming in and out of my room. It typically started at 4:30 a.m. for blood draws which were analyzed to ensure that indicators were heading the right way. The first phlebotomist would draw blood from a vein, which was relatively easy as the blood could be taken from an existing intra-venal site. No big deal.

The second phlebotomist would jab a scalpel into the radial artery on my wrist to get the sample of bright red arterial blood to evaluate lung function by analyzing the arterial blood gases. He would usually make an accurate incision first time, and the torture would be over quickly.

Sometimes, it was not so easy. The first jab would miss the artery, and the phlebotomist would dig around a little more until he found it. The pain was excruciating. I had to steel myself every morning not to scream in agony. I smiled at the irony of not feeling so much pain from the transplant surgery, only to be punished by a blood draw. To add insult to injury, the blood draws always took place daily before 5:00 a.m.

The nurses would buzz in and out of my room until doctors' rounds at 7:30 a.m. When the transplant surgeon entered my room, he was accompanied by a phalanx of younger doctors. He would go straight into asking specific questions and looking to his team for rapid answers, while barely acknowledging the patient. His eyes darted over the dials and indicators clustered around the room. For him, it was vital that there was no sign of infection from the surgery and that the delicately balanced immuno-suppressant drugs were doing their job. The next most important thing was that the patient was getting out of bed.

"Is he walking?" the surgeon asked impatiently, looking at everyone in the room except me.

Walking was not an issue for me. I walked with determination, albeit at a pace that an elderly tortoise would find frustrating. The nurses would vouch that I was regularly creeping around the pulmonary unit, albeit at glacial speed. The staff had helpfully mapped out the one-eighth of a mile route along the corridors of the unit, and I proudly recorded each step on a wall chart. The surgeon seemed to relax when he realized that, yes, I was indeed walking.

One morning, I overheard him remonstrating with a patient in the room next door. His voice was raised as he was obviously irritated by reports that she was not walking at all. "If you don't walk, you are going to waste the lungs. Should I have given them to someone else?" he asked pointedly.

That was enough to galvanize the patient into action. I saw her out of bed and in the corridor moments later, reluctantly shuffling along the corridor.

The morning chest x-rays were next. I was hoisted into a wheel chair by a cheerful orderly, who would load up all my boxes and drips, and whip me along the hospital corridors at break-neck speed to the x-ray unit. As I was not allowed to eat or drink anything and my only nutrition came from the glucose drip, I was losing more body weight. Whenever I left my hospital room, I would start to shake with cold due to low body fat. I would ask for two blankets to keep me warm during these early morning spins.

68

After the x-rays, I was returned to my room. I was usually aware that breakfast was being served to other patients. There was no breakfast for me - my designation was *nil per os* - due to the risk of fluid aspiration. People often complain about the quality of hospital food, but I never did. From my isolated vantage point, it looked and smelled delicious.

The doctors were pleased with my progress. Tubes were being removed and my accessory pile was shrinking like discarded flotsam. The doctors were talking openly that perhaps I could get out the following Monday, which would exactly hit my ten-day target. I was still taking regular walks around the corridors. Eighteen laps were one mile, and I could usually chalk up two miles at a time.

At the beginning of the week, I needed a nurse to come with me during my walks. I was slowly getting better at walking, my breathing was clearer, and I was more adept at guiding the two stands-on-wheels that held all my boxes.

I always wore my running shoes, so I could walk in comfort without using hospital slippers. The nurses and doctors found it amusing that I would rest on my bed only sporting the ignominious hospital gown and red running shoes between circuits.

Although drainage tubes were being removed from my chest, I had to have one additional tube inserted into my stomach, a common procedure at Duke following transplant. The doctors were waiting until a few days after the transplant surgery for me to recover some strength before inserting the feeding tube[12].

A week after the transplant, the doctors quickly and painlessly inserted the tube six inches above my belly button. It would leave a hole in my skin but, by this point, I was oblivious to more scarring. As I was partially awake, I could talk to the nurse who was at my side during the procedure. I remember the nurse saying that survival of what I was going through was nine-tenths mental attitude. I laid back and felt the pressure sensation on my stomach as the feeding tube was put in place. At least I

12  Percutaneous endoscopic gastrostomy (PEG) tube.

would be able to consume liquids through the tube. Zander was excited that I would be left with a "bullet hole" in my stomach.

There is a lot of time to think when you are in the hospital, especially at night, when you are propped up in bed and cannot sleep. I made a mental list of the things I wanted to do when I got back to health. I needed something physically challenging that would help in my recovery, something that would exercise all muscle groups, as well as providing a robust cardiovascular work-out. The idea of getting back to swimming began to percolate in my mind.

One of the preparatory talks we received pre-transplant was from a double-lung transplant recipient, Tiffany Christensen. She had received a new set of lungs in 2000, then a second set in 2002 when her body went into rejection. She has since dedicated herself to patient advocacy healthcare issues through her books, videos, and talks[13].

She had suffered from cystic fibrosis since the age of six months and was enduring all the challenges of lung transplant. Based on her exposure to the medical world, she was uniquely qualified to make some insightful observations.

One comment particularly resonated. She said that the way she coped with such vast medical attention throughout her life was that she "gave in" to the process as opposed to fighting it. By giving in, she certainly didn't mean giving up on her will to live or her desire to beat illness. By giving in, she meant surrendering to the relentless process of medical care, doctors' visits, treatments, blood draws, x-rays, and all the rest of the steps in her on-going care. She had made a conscious effort to stop trying to analyze the situation and to go with the flow of her treatments. She had mentally handed herself over to her medical team to take over and let go of all the extra stuff that might impede her recovery. Her job was to focus her full attention and energy on becoming well again.

Tiffany's approach is remarkably grounded. To her, a cure is one possible outcome to illness, but patients may find

---

13  www.sickgirlspeaks.com

themselves distressed if a cure is their only objective and they do not get there. Being fully cured is elusive. Tiffany advocates a spirit of acceptance enmeshed with practical strategies to make life better, regardless of the physical outcome. I have always found it helpful to keep her words in mind.

## Speed bump

The axiom of lung transplant is that everyone hits a speed bump at some point. Mine came a week after the surgery. Two of the largest chest tubes were ready to be removed. The fluid flowing out of the tubes was yellow in color, not the bleeding red of earlier in the week, which was a good sign. Two doctors came into my room and announced that they were going to take out the two remaining chest tubes. I was asked to lean over to one side and take some deep breaths as they removed the first tube.

One, two, three. I felt a sharp tug on my right side as the doctors yanked out the plastic drainage tubes. I stifled a cry, as the tubes grated over raw flesh as they came out. The nurses applied a dressing on the open wound and taped it up. I breathed a sigh of relief. The worst was over.

I settled down in bed for the next hour or so. I did not feel bad, just a little beaten up. As time went on, I felt light headed and a little dizzy. The nurse who regularly checked my blood pressure noticed that it was low. She mentioned that said she would keep an eye on it. I felt a peculiar dampness on the bed sheets beneath me but, as I had felt so many odd sensations recently, I ignored it.

A short time later, a doctor came to check on the wound dressing from which the right-side chest tube had been pulled. She asked me to roll over onto my left side, so she could access the dressing. Even from my twisted vantage point, I could see her eyes widen in alarm. The dressing and sheets around me were soaked bright red. She rushed from the room, returning seconds later with a colleague, and the two of them hurriedly reapplied the dressing to stem the flow of blood.

The nurse scuttled back into the room and took my blood pressure again. It was very low. Now I really felt light headed and lay back in bed. Moments later, a doctor, who I later found out was the on-call transplant surgeon, strode into the room, and took charge. He came around to my head and said loudly, "Gavin, can you hear me?" I could hear him perfectly, but I could hardly respond. I felt so weak.

"Yes," I croaked, inaudibly, my lips barely moving. He looked at me uncomprehendingly.

"Put the tubes back in," he barked at the two hovering doctors. The abrupt re-insertion of the chest tube into the raw flesh hole in my right side was even more excruciating as the removal had been. I breathed in and out exactly as the doctors instructed, but it did not lessen the pain. Usually, I have a reasonably high pain tolerance, but today was savage.

I had lost a lot of blood through a ruptured blood vessel – too much blood. The nurses rushed to prepare for an emergency blood transfusion, and I lay back and let them do their work. I felt like a bewildered spectator watching a macabre play, where all I could do was stand by as the drama unfolded. That was the only day when I thought that my number might be up. It was a somber time. To add insult to injury, I was back on supplemental oxygen.

After the blood transfusion, the surgeon came back to talk to me. He was a much friendlier version of the original surgeon. He was almost certain that a blood vessel that had been kept closed by the inserted chest tube had ruptured, he said. The bleeding was caused by the removal of the tube which had opened the blood vessel. He explained that the only option was to open my chest again and tie off the ruptured blood vessel. He said that he could perform the surgery the first thing the next morning. He wasn't asking for my permission, rather just telling me what had to be done.

I had a restless night. The nurses performed another blood transfusion before I went to sleep at 10:00 p.m. The human body contains about five-and-a-half-liters of blood, and the nurses told me that they had transfused four liters into my body.

The next morning, I had the usual blood draws at the crack of dawn, but no x-ray. The same cheerful orderly came to collect me around 7:00 a.m., transferred me to a gurney and wheeled me to the operating room.

Before I knew it, I was waking up in the post-operative recovery room. A surgeon who I had not met before came to see me. He said the procedure had gone well, and that as soon as they had opened my chest, they could see the leaking blood vessel, with blood literally chugging out. They had tied a knot in it (yes, really, that's what he said) and that it should be fine now. Not so prosaic, but effective. He emphasized it was vitally important that I used my pulmonary blowing device. "Use it every thirty minutes for the next twelve hours," he advised.

I doubt the nurses ever witnessed such alacritous use of that little blowing device over the following few hours.

By the ninth day of my stay at Duke Hospital, I was feeling stronger. The surgeon said I could go home the next day. I was anxious to leave and to get back to the hotel that we called home from home in North Carolina. The risk of hospital-acquired infection is ever-present and is especially dangerous to the immunosuppressed, so the sooner you leave, the better.

The next challenge was to get to grips with the feeding tube routine and my daily medications. Admittedly, I hadn't been paying as close attention to the nurses as I could have as the array of daily medicines were administered at precise times.

Food came first. Each night, two or three cans of artificial liquid food were poured into a transparent bag on a stand at the bedside. A mini-pump pushed the liquid through the narrow tube connected to my stomach tube. I was surprised how little sensation I felt as the liquid slowly flowed into my stomach. Obviously, there was no taste, as the food was going straight to my stomach, but I did not get any sensation of "fullness" either.

The medicines came next. I knew from the pre-operation briefings that the discipline of taking medication on time was non-negotiable. Up to the point of discharge from the hospital, all the medications had been administered by the nurses. I had also become diabetic since the transplant due to receiving high dosages of methylprednisolone, an anti-inflammatory and immunosuppressant drug, during the surgery. It was time I learned how to do everything, including how to self-inject the insulin. I had a sheet of the medications, and an order was placed at the local pharmacy for the prescriptions.

**Threat of rejection**

One of the biggest fears of any organ transplant recipient is chronic rejection. The most important medicines are the immunosuppressants, which suppress the body's immune system to allow the new organs to survive. Immunosuppressants must be taken daily. I took, and still take, three daily immunosuppression drugs[14]. We needed to get organized.

I was given a pill box with twenty-eight compartments - seven columns, one for each day of the week - and four rows. This box would ensure that I knew which drugs to take at which time. I could not miss a dose, so had to ensure that I carefully tracked what I had taken, and that prescriptions were refilled several days before they ran out. I also have a small four-compartment box for each day's drugs.

The body's immune system protects you from foreign invaders such as bacteria and viruses. White blood cells called lymphocytes detect the foreign invaders and signal your immune system to attack them. Transplanted lungs are exclusively made up of "foreign" cells, so your immune system, which cannot tell the difference between good invaders (the transplanted lungs) and bad invaders (bacteria and viruses), will try to attack and destroy them.

To reduce such attacks, the transplanted lungs are matched for blood and tissue type prior to the transplant. However, even with a good match, the body's immune system thinks that the new organ is a foreign invader. Immunosuppressant drugs are prescribed to "slow down" your immune system. Even with the anti-rejection medications, we were told that it is common for transplant recipients to have at least one episode of acute rejection. Rejection is most common during the first few months following the transplant, but it can occur at any time. Small bouts

---

14  Tacrolimus (3mg x 2), azathioprine (100mg), and prednisone (5mg)

of rejection were not too worrisome and could be stopped if detected and treated immediately.

In the months following my transplant, I had three episodes of rejection. After a scheduled bronchoscopy, I would get a call from my lung transplant coordinator. My heart would sink when I heard the news. The very word "rejection" was enough to send a chill up my spine. However, although it is scary, rejection does not mean that the new lungs have failed. Acute rejection is treated by blasting the body with high dosages of the steroid, methylprednisolone. My three episodes were treated successfully. It is a constant reminder that you cannot take your lungs for granted.

Although my immune system is, of course, weakened, I have found ways to cope by taking basic precautions, such as regular hand washing and staying away from people who are sick. Ailments such as the common cold tend to last longer and be more severe for people with compromised immune systems.

Each morning, I load up a four-compartment pill box with the medicines I need for the day and carry it around in my pocket. My cell phone's alarm rings at 9:30 a.m. to remind me of the morning dose, and I remember to take the later ones. I seldom get the dosages or timings wrong. For the first post-transplant year, I felt resentful at being tied to the unforgiving drug regimen. As time passed, I got more used to it and soon the resentment left, leaving me with just another routine task like teeth-brushing.

On discharge from the hospital after an eleven-day stay - just one day off my goal - we headed back to the hotel via the pharmacy to fill prescriptions. I still had six weeks ahead of me in the rehabilitation program, but it was a delectable feeling to leave the confines of the hospital and breathe in the outside air. Just the simple act of breathing and smelling the pine wood of nearby bushes made me feel overwhelmingly happy and optimistic.

I will take the immunosuppression medication for the rest of my life. The drill was inculcated during my hospital stay. No matter how good you feel, they would say, there is no leeway. Do not stop taking the prescribed daily medications. Never, ever.

I am still surprised at how often people ask, "How long do you have to keep taking the medications?" They believe that surely your body will be able to cope on its own at some point after the operation.

Unfortunately, that's not how it works. Your body never gets used to the transplanted organ. Sometimes, it is almost comical to be asked the question. Even my primary care physician, whom I consulted some years later about a non-lung issue, looked at my list of daily drugs, and asked incredulously, "Are you still taking all these drugs?"

Mind you, this was the same physician who, when I told him I felt fine despite my lung issue, quipped with a grin, "That's like saying, Mrs. Lincoln, apart from the obvious, how was the rest of the show?" Very droll. He probably needs to get out more.

## Discharged

The first few nights out of the hospital were also tough going. I was still reeling from the impact of the two surgeries, the side effects of the drugs, and the fact that I had not slept well in the hospital. Day and night merged together, and I found I was awake at night, and exhausted during the day. It took several days for my body clock to adjust.

There is also some trepidation at being discharged from the hospital, as you no longer have medical staff to help and answer questions. Julie's background in medicine and pharmaceuticals was invaluable in navigating the maze of terminology and prescriptions.

I took medications in liquid form in the hospital, as I had so many intravenous entry points into my body. Now I was no longer in hospital, I had to take the pills orally. Because I was not allowed to eat or drink anything by mouth, apart from the medications, I was still only getting nutrition through the stomach tube. I had to take a tiny quantity of specially prepared "thick liquid" which was awkwardly ingested through the corner of my mouth. The orange flavored liquid protected my lungs from any damage that could be caused by ingesting liquids of water-like viscosity.

Having become a recent diabetic meant a routine of stabbing my finger, measuring my blood sugar levels, and injecting the right dose of insulin. I had no experience of diabetes, as I did not have it before the transplant, and did not know anyone first hand who had it. Once I understood the management regime, I had a huge respect for diabetes sufferers who deal with the invasive routine every day. In my case, I was only a diabetic for three months until my body began to regulate its own level of insulin again.

A fundamental belief at Duke was the role of exercise in the healing process. The Center for Living rehabilitation program was the focal point. It was a large gymnasium-type building on the fringes of the Duke campus, with an indoor running track and exercise equipment. When transplant candidates first arrive at Duke for evaluation, they are told about the importance of the Center for Living to their successful outcome. They are signed up for their exercise program regardless of their current fitness level. Some transplant candidates are overweight and are informed that they need to lose weight. Others have never exercised regularly before and are just out of shape. But everyone is expected to exercise.

The day prior to my discharge from the hospital, the surgeon told me that I was to show up at the Center for Living the very next day. I knew the lung transplant recipients like me were scheduled for the afternoon slot and were expected to complete a six-week course of at least four days a week. The session was split into four exercise blocks, supervised by a squad of respiratory therapists. The next afternoon, I arrived feeling like I had been hit by a bus but laced up my running shoes anyway and reported for duty.

I had lost weight in hospital and my legs were scrawny twigs. Under normal circumstances, exercise is my favorite pastime, and I have always considered myself to be one of the fittest people I know. But today, standing at the exercise machines, waiting my turn for the leg press to push out twenty pounds[15], I felt unbelievably feeble. Of course, we were not allowed to do upper body exercises, but leg exercises were expected. I finished as many leg presses as I could and felt queasy. I leaned over to one of the respiratory therapists.

---

15  9kg

"I'm feeling sick. I'm not sure if I can do any more." After all, it was one day after I was out of the hospital.

"Not to worry," she said, sunnily. She held up a waste paper bin and handed it to me. "Here is something to vomit into. Keep it beside you."

I finished the session by walking slowly around the running track. By 4:30 p.m., I was knackered.

After the first session, the daily rehabilitation routines became easier as my body slowly got stronger. It was satisfying to make my way, walking however slowly, around the track without an oxygen tank.

"How long before I can run?" I asked. Truthfully, I could not have broken into a run to escape from a charging grizzly bear, but I liked to ask. We'll check and get back to you, they would say.

I exercised every day, except Tuesdays, when I went to the Duke clinic for lab tests, which took up most of the day. I would get a chest x-ray, blood drawn for analysis, and pulmonary function tests (PFTs). I had an appointment with one of the Duke pulmonologists. I usually saw the same doctor, who would look at my lab results, listen to my breathing, and tap on my back. He was generally satisfied with my progress. I was always relieved when the consultation was over.

The PFTs were one of the most important parts of the assessment. By blowing into a tube at full force, the doctors could assess lung function.[16] Before my transplant, I dreaded the PFTs. It was like going into a high school exam, knowing that you had not studied at all. My performance was always pitiful. When I first consulted a pulmonologist in 2004, my lung function had fallen to sixty percent level of the predicted level. By 2007, my lung function had plummeted to thirty percent. No wonder I felt constantly ill.

But not anymore. Now I could push out a hurricane-force exhale that would send the measurements soaring. The PFTs

---

16 Pulmonary Function Tests (PFTs) measure the first expiratory volume of forceful exhalation in the first second ($FEV_1$) and forced vital capacity, the amount of air forcibly exhaled from the lungs after taking the deepest breath possible (FVC)

showed my lung function at sixty percent. Every week, it rose by a couple of percentage points. I actually looked forward to the test and savored my burgeoning lung function.

I had one more surgical hurdle to clear. As part of Duke's medical treatment protocol, they recommended that each lung transplant recipient receives a so-called "stomach wrap" if there is any evidence of gastroesophageal reflux disease[17], or acid reflux disease, the chronic symptoms produced by abnormal reflux in the esophagus.

Many lung transplant recipients suffer from some degree of acid reflux. It is more than deleterious, it can be life-threatening. Stomach acid can be aspirated up through the esophagus and into the lungs, causing aspiration pneumonia. To pre-empt this problem, the surgeons would perform a stomach wrap[18]. The upper part of the stomach is wrapped around the inferior part of the esophagus and stitched into place. This reinforces the closing function of the lower esophageal sphincter, so whenever the stomach contracts, it also closes off the esophagus instead of squeezing stomach acids into it. This prevents the reflux of gastric acid back up the esophagus and, potentially, into the lungs. The practical result was that I could no longer easily swallow large pieces of food.

I was scheduled to go back into the hospital to get the stomach wrap – an irreversible procedure - in the following weeks. The idea did not exactly fill me with eager anticipation, but I knew it was another necessary step on the road to recovery.

## Wrapping-up

I had the stomach wrap surgery in mid-May 2008. Compared to the lung transplant, the stomach surgery was a cinch. It only required a four-day hospital stay.

When I woke up from the anesthetic, my stomach was quite bruised, and I felt as if I had been rabbit punched several times.

---

17  GERD in the United States, but GORD in the UK, due to the different spelling of oesophagus for obscure etymological reasons
18  Medically, a Nissen fundoplication

The surgery had been laparoscopic, so there were only small puncture wounds. I compared everything now to the transplant operation. Stomach surgery? Easy-peasy.

I was still "eating" through the stomach feeding tube, so was anticipating the stomach-wrap surgery as a stepping stone to the resumption of eating solid food. On my discharge, I could take "clear liquids" by mouth for two weeks. Practically, that meant water and chicken broth. Oddly, I did not feel hungry. I stuck to the nightly regime of filling up my feeding bag at 6:00 p.m. and let it run, its little motor whirring, until the next morning.

Technically, I was taking in enough calories to keep me fueled but it was not enough to replace the lost weight. I weighed myself every morning, but I did not gain much weight. After two weeks, I progressed to "dark liquids," so at least I could enjoy a cup of black coffee.

You do not realize – until you don't do it – just how much time you spend on the whole food and eating thing: shopping, preparing, eating, and cleaning up.

Although I was ecstatic to be going home, I was also a little nervous to be so far away from my medical experts at Duke. I knew I would have to sever the cord at some point, and that I could do so just three months after my transplant was a considerable achievement. I thanked all the respiratory therapists profusely on my last afternoon. They seemed so proud when one of their lung recipients graduated from the six-week program.

"Oh, almost forgot," one therapist offered. "It's twelve weeks."

"Twelve weeks?"

"Until you can start running again. Good luck!"

To be on the safe side, I wore a surgical mask during the flight to Colorado. On Southwest Airlines, passengers choose their own seats on boarding and generally window and aisle are the most sought-after. Funnily enough, if you are already on the aircraft, and wearing a surgical mask, no one wants to sit next to you. They just assume you are harboring something unpleasant and contagious. I resisted the temptation to point out that I was not protecting them from me, but rather me from them.

I had been away from home for over four months. When I left, I had been tethered to the oxygen concentrator and oxygen tubes ran throughout the house. Now, I was breathing on my own, and felt great.

Julie had already sent the oxygen concentrator machine back to the oxygen company, along with the piles of portable oxygen tanks that had been stacked in the garage. I was nervous at first. What happens if I need supplemental oxygen again? Maybe we should keep everything for a little longer, just in case? But it was a good decision. It represented a Crossing of the Rubicon that allowed me to move forward and focus on the future, as opposed to looking over my shoulder.

I guess I thought that once I got home, everything would be back to normal. But my body was still adjusting to the medications. I felt more tired than usual and I was still painfully thin. I still used the feeding tube at night until I got a nod from the physicians to start on solid foods several weeks later.

An exercise routine was key to my recovery. It was recommended to walk one to two miles daily, five days a week, along with other arm and shoulder exercises at the gym. I used the local park where I could choose from circuits of one or two miles and made sure that I completed my regimen every day.

As the weeks passed, I could walk further and further, as I felt myself getting stronger. Once the stomach feeding tube was removed in August, I headed to the local swimming pool as soon as the wounds fully healed. I initially started swimming only two, four or six lengths at a time. Within two months, I could cover half a mile. It was the feeling I had waited so long for: the sensation of my lungs expanding and contracting with the exertion of exercise and inhaling without coughing and spluttering. It felt magical.

My walking had progressed to a slow jog, and I started going faster, perhaps imperceptibly so. Our family dog was particularly pleased when I started to jog again, and I delighted in the simplicity of running slowly around the neighborhood with my panting friend.

It was around that time that I decided to shoot for a sprint-distance triathlon the following year. I have found that setting a specific goal is the best source of motivation. From my monthly check-ups at Duke, I knew that my lung function was increasing at each visit. It was now around eighty-five percent of the predicted level.

By December, I could jog comfortably, and I could feel some mass coming back to my atrophied muscles. The looming event motivated my training through the winter months, sun, rain or snow.

As the event approached, I had a clinic visit at Duke Hospital at the end of March. I was pleased that my pulmonary function tests were at an all-time high of ninety-eight percent. I had shaken off an episode of rejection from December. I had been training six days a week for the past few months. Ever since the transplant, I had felt tired, especially when I finished exercising. But I knew that cardiovascular exercise was the best medicine for my lungs. Just keep going, I said to myself.

I completed the triathlon in April 2009. It was the first psychological mountain I had to climb. It was a typical Colorado spring day – a beautiful clear sky, crisp air, and low temperatures.

I held my own in the swimming leg of four-hundred meters in the pool at full tilt, was slower on the twelve-mile bike leg - probably my weakest event - and staggered over the finish line after the three-mile run. In a field of several hundred competitors, I finished dead last. It felt wonderful.

# CHAPTER SEVEN: MOUNTAINS TO CLIMB

*Follow your passion, stay true to yourself, never follow someone else's path unless you're in the woods and you're lost, and you see a path then by all means you should follow that.*

- Ellen Degeneres

**Six years post-transplant: finding challenges is not so hard**

There isn't a manual for post-transplant life. You just have to get on with things. It is difficult to completely forget about the transplant, as the daily immunosuppression regimen is ever-present. I take six separate daily prescriptions. Monthly prescriptions run out and need to be refilled. Somehow, they work their way out of synch so there is not a single refill date. It seems like a constant chore of calling the pharmacy for refills, picking them up, and requesting prescription renewals.

The twice-daily immunosuppressant drugs are the most critical to get right. Too much means an accelerated impact on other organs, such as the kidneys. Too little means the immune system may not be sufficiently suppressed, which could lead to rejection. It is a delicate balance. Blood draws are also needed every month to check the drug's level. I mark my calendar and drop by the local hospital before work.

Venipuncture, the drawing of blood from a vein, sounds ominous. Historically, techniques such as leeches to draw blood from a hapless patient, as well as bloodletting to remove toxins, were applied. Happily, nowadays, a phlebotomist (from the Greek *phlebo-*, meaning "relating to a blood vessel", and *-tomia*, meaning "cutting of") can draw blood in about sixty seconds.

But combining "blood" and "cutting" is never good. Some people are affected by trypanophobia – the extreme fear of needles or injections. I don't have that, but no matter how often I have blood drawn, I still wince when the needle goes in. I couldn't imagine anyone actually enjoys being punctured - until I met a phlebotomist called John.

John's arms and neck above his neckline were covered in tattoos. Maybe his whole body was too, I don't know. When I asked him about them, he told me that his previous job had been a tattoo artist, and he had also dabbled as a part-time acupuncturist. A move into phlebotomy seemed like a logical career progression, he chuckled. Plus, the pay was more reliable. And, he added with a smile, he was a diabetic, so he had more than a passing affiliation with needles.

I resign myself to the processing time – checking-in, waiting my turn, being verified in the computer system – my name, my date of birth, my address, for the zillionth time - waiting for the phlebotomist, pulling up my sleeve, getting the blood drawn, being bandaged up, pulling down my sleeve, heading back to the car, waiting two days, emailing Duke to make sure they have got the results, and adjusting, sometimes, the number of capsules I take.

You must live your life and manage the medications. I describe this part as finding challenges, allowing yourself some wins, and tapping into sources of inspiration.

Fortunately, finding challenges is not so hard, especially in Colorado. For example, the American Lung Association organizes an annual fundraising series called the Fight for Air Climb. Who could resist such a fabulously-named challenge? The event involves selecting a prominent city skyscraper and inviting sponsored enthusiasts to leg it up the stairwell – hundreds of steps, dozens of floors - on a Sunday morning. Funds raised support research, education, and patient programs to help people - who literally fight for air daily - impacted by asthma, COPD, lung cancer, air pollution, and other respiratory diseases.

In Denver, the climb takes place in the Republic Plaza building with fifty-six floors and 1,098 steps. Zander, Riley, and I participated in 2011 and 2012. Both times were harder than I had anticipated.

As we filed towards the stairwell door in the building's basement at the designated time for our second ascent, there was a lot of excitement. Teams from local companies with matching t-shirts, police officers, crews of firefighters laden down with equipment, and individual athletes laughed and chattered with each other as they got ready for the lung-busting ascent.

We have a standing family joke about the metaphoric "lung transplant card." We would often hike in the foothills of the Rocky Mountains when I was recovering from the transplant. I would invariably lag from exertion and the effects of altitude. One day, Riley looked back and said, "Come on, Dad. Don't play the lung transplant card!" I have really never made excuses for myself about my transplant and physical limitations, but Riley would invariably tease me all the same. I had to keep up to avoid the dreaded transplant card accusation.

As usual with these events, the three of us started together. And, as usual, as we went through the doorway, Zander and Riley darted off up the stairs, their skinny legs racing as they disappeared around the first corner.

"See you at the top, Dad!" they shouted. "Remember, no transplant card!"

I always set off too quickly, over-eager to show off my cardiovascular prowess. The first, second, and third flight of stairs were deceptively straightforward and confirmed my self-assurance. This is easy, I thought, as I bounded up two and three steps at a time. But my respiratory system had other ideas. It could not replace oxygen fast enough and the oxygen debt had to be repaid. It slammed on the brakes. I ground to a halt mid-step and convulsed in respiratory distress, desperately gasping for breath.

Two young women came up behind me. "Are you alright?" they asked, concerned. I wordlessly waived them past, mouthing that I was fine, really. Only the wheezing sound of asphyxiation came out as I slumped on the steps. Oh, the Fight for Air Climb is aptly named, I thought again.

More climbers came up behind me. "Are you sure you are okay?" "Yes, no worries," I replied. "No need to call the paramedics, really." I attempted to cover my embarrassment by pretending to adjust my waist band water bottle. These things really do come loose easily. I was fooling no one.

After a few minutes, my breathing regulated itself enough that I could carry on, but at a more sedate pace. Twenty-nine minutes later, taking one step at a time, I had reached the top. Zander and Riley were already there, of course, excitedly looking at the city from the vantage view point of the fifty-sixth floor, eating chips and swigging water.

"Hey, Dad! What took you so long?"

## Finding balance

As a life-long runner, I always wanted to get back to running post-transplant. Although I pushed for medical permission, and was medically cleared, once I started to run I felt stiff and sore. My running pace was little more than a walking-shuffle. I felt despondent at my performance.

I also dwelled on comments from Duke about the anti-inflammatory drug, prednisone, which was one of my daily mandatories. "Bone-poison" was how one physician described it. Even with daily doses of five milligrams – the dose I had been on since my transplant – studies show that it is often associated with reduced bone density and increased risk of hip and vertebral fractures. The obvious question to the doctor in the early days of recovery was "do I really need to keep taking this drug?"

"Yes," was the response. "Take it every day and don't stop taking it under any circumstances."

Activities that are recommended for people at greater risk of osteopenia/osteoporosis include strength training, weight-bearing aerobic activities, especially, as well as flexibility exercises. The trick is to find time to balance the various types of exercise. It's also important that non-weight bearing aerobic activities, as beneficial as they are for your overall health, are not the entirety of your exercise program. Non-weight bearing sports - like cycling, yoga, and, of course, swimming - have many benefits, but they don't provide a healthy load that your bones need.[19]

Weight-bearing aerobic activities - moving around on your feet - work on the bones in the legs, hips and lower spine, which

---

19 At this point, I should probably make the following statement: everyone should consult their medical doctor prior to embarking on any physical exercise program. There, I said it.

helps to slow mineral loss. They also provide cardiovascular benefits by boosting the heart and circulatory system. My checklist includes walking whenever I can, running – both outside and on a treadmill at the gym - and sometimes other gym machines like elliptical trainer or stair climber.

Strength training includes the use of free weights or your body weight to strengthen major muscle groups, as well as maintaining bone density.

Pre-transplant, I parked as closely as possible to a store's entrance, as I could not walk very far. Post-transplant, I jumped at any opportunity to exercise, so I would often park at the furthest extremity of the parking lot and jog to and from the store. I even ran inside the grocery store for a time, until it seemed like a real possibility I would be mistaken for a fleeing shoplifter and brought down by an over-zealous security guard.

**The deep end**

At this point, apart from occasional visits to the local pool, I hadn't really returned to swimming. I was still skeptical about the health risks posed by the pool surroundings in my immunocompromised state and thought I should focus on more gravity-oriented activities. The flexibility part of the equation was secondary.

But try as I might, I couldn't energize my old enthusiasm for running. It seemed tedious, hard, even boring.

Determined to push on, I found an online story about a double- lung recipient who was competing in Ironman triathlons. In the online video, the camera followed him as he ran. I could see with my own eyes that he was road-running fluidly and steadily. It was an epiphany for me, my own lightbulb moment. I could see what was possible with transplanted lungs.

I looked Scott Johnson up on social media and sent him a message to ask if we could talk. He readily agreed. When we connected, I explained that I was having a mental block about exercising. I knew it was important, I said, but there were so many obstacles. My excuses came thick and fast: prednisone and joint damage, my lack of running fluidity, not being able to breathe as well as before. You name it, I had an excuse for it.

I doubt if Scott knows how much help he gave me on that short phone call that afternoon. "I just run," he said. "I don't worry about all that stuff."

If I had been moving, I would have stopped in my tracks. Don't worry about all that stuff? Was that possible? But what if I tried it? What was the worst that could happen?

After thanking Scott for his time, I literally hung up, found and dusted off my running shoes, went out the front door in what I was wearing, and started running down the street. I felt suddenly unshackled. It was the perfect metaphor I needed to clear away psychological obstacles that were impeding my physiological abilities.

Around that time, the American Transplant Foundation put me in touch with Russ Cupps, a local firefighter. He was training to compete in the Denver *Rock n' Roll Marathon* that fall for *Team Transplant*, the event fundraising arm of the American Transplant Foundation.

Russ was the first person I had ever met who was an altruistic kidney donor. He had donated one of his kidneys to a stranger. And he was training to run a marathon. Russ asked me if I would run the half-marathon relay event with his wife, Angela, to raise funds for organ transplant awareness. I readily agreed, even though I had not run anything close to six miles in years. It provided a wonderful motivational milestone.

On race-day, I ran the first leg of the relay, so about six of the thirteen miles. The relay baton was an actual drummer's drumstick, which I proudly held onto until I passed it over to Angela at the almost half-way mark. The lighthearted trait of a *Rock n' Roll* event is the live music that is performed at each mile marker. Once you passed one band, you listened closely for the distant music of the next band at the next mile marker. It was an entertaining motivator.

The mantra in my head was "just keep going." My running pace was interminably slow at around fifteen-minute miles, but I avoided dropping down to a walk, which was my goal for the run when I handed over the baton. I had hit my target of actually running from start to finish in a running race. It was one of my small athletic wins and I felt utterly gratified.

## Accept inspiration

"Why all this focus on running?" Julie used to say in exasperation. "Do something else."

I knew she was right and that I should have been happy with my lack of limitations. Maybe I should accept that my best running days were behind me? Inspiration often comes from unlikely sources. Mine came from Will Smith, the American actor, producer, rapper, comedian, and songwriter. In 2007, *Newsweek* called him "the most powerful actor in Hollywood". Smith has been nominated for five Golden Globe Awards, two Academy Awards and has won four Grammy Awards. In 2010 he won an award at the 2005 Kids Choice Awards and gave a forceful speech on his two self-identified keys to life: running and reading. Reading of course provides an endless source of knowledge and inspiration. But of running, he yelled:

"Why running? When you're out there and you're running, there's a little person that talks to you and that little person says, "Oh I'm tired. My lungs are about to pop. I'm so hurt. I'm so tired. There's no way I can possibly continue." And you want to quit. If you learn how to defeat that person when you're running, you will learn how to not quit when things get hard in your life."

I believe that running also embodies two combined techniques that have contributed to my recovery: goal setting and being motivated by others. The goals of the open-water swims gave me focus and motivation. Training alongside other athletes in a pool intensified the motivation, as well as providing camaraderie.

If I covered the bases of strength and weight-bearing aerobic exercise, that left flexibility. As a young athlete, I used to go through the motions of warm-up stretching before a rugby game or swimming competition, but never felt it was very useful. I could always touch my toes, so why stretch any further?

As my lung function deteriorated in the mid-2000s, and I was coughing and trying to find respiratory relief, as well as a desire to find an exercise that was not cardiovascular, the path led somewhat inexorably to yoga. I tried out several different types, but did not participate often enough to accrue any real joint mobility benefits. *Bikram* yoga was one of the bearable classes, as it was in a hot room, and my feeble flexibility often improved marginally with the benefit of warm muscles.

I also participated in an *Astanga* class for no other better reason than I had read a newspaper article that described it as the exercise of choice of the singer, Madonna. My shallowness apart, the class did provide a rigorous workout, but I could not stop coughing, and felt I was disturbing the flow of the class. I did not go back.

I probably attended no more than three or four yoga classes every year and was usually one of the minority of male participants with similarly limited ranges of motion cowering at the back of the room. My balance and flexibility were generally miserable. A yoga instructor would invariably approach as if to tweak a basic pose, then seem to change her mind, and move on to another class participant. I wondered if my yoga strictures were either verging on perfection or were so far from the mark that any attempt at correction was futile. No prizes for guessing which one was accurate. In fact, one of the few recurring comments I did receive from the instructor was in response to my habitually contorted visage was something like, "You can relax your face!" Not really the flexibility I had in mind.

There is little doubt that moving your joints through their full range of motion helps your muscles work well, and the breathing and meditative elements of the practice made sense to me. I persevered even though, by the end of a class, I usually felt more beaten up and humiliated than graceful and lithe. I continued to be intrigued by the use of breath, as well as meditation that is central to yoga practice, to overcome physical limitations. In theory, yoga sounded exactly what I should be doing. In practice, I can honestly say that I hated it.

## Boulder and bolder

If health and well-being is your goal, Colorado is a good place to start. With approximately three hundred days of sunshine per year, it has more people who exercise per capita and fewer overweight people than any other US state. The city of Boulder is often called the country's happiest city because of its repeated ranking as the best city for well-being. With a population of one hundred thousand people, it is estimated to have around ninety-three thousand bicycles. It is also widely believed that bike paths are snow plowed before roads in winter. And, of course, it is one of the nation's best cities for running and triathlon training.

The arrival of spring means longer daylight, warm weather, and blossoming trees. It also means the imminence of my all-time favorite day and event of the year: Memorial Day's Bolder Boulder. To the uninitiated, the Bolder Boulder is just an annual ten-kilometer road run. But it is more than that. It is a celebration. Over fifty-four thousand runners, walkers, and wheelchair racers participated in 2017, making it one of the largest ten-kilometer road races in the country.

The festival atmosphere covers the entire course, with residents playing music and handing out drinks to passing runners, squads of cheerleaders, belly dancers, bagpipers, live bands, and well-wishers lining the streets. The event itself is one of jaw-dropping proportions and breathtaking aura. The atmosphere of well-being and positivity is infectious and overwhelming, even more so considering that so many tens of thousands of people, of as many sizes, ages, races, nationalities and backgrounds as you can imagine, who are running six miles.

The final part of the race is a victory lap at the University of Colorado's Folsom Field – home of the famed Buffaloes college football team – to a steadily filling stadium. The elite runners set off later than the amateur athletes, so they arrive in the stadium – now packed with race finishers and their families – to a tight finish and rapturous applause. Parachutists land on the field to honor the five branches of the armed forces.

My running pace is a little slower than the elites. I have been in the United States for the past fifteen Bolder Boulders and have missed only two events: the year before and the year after my lung transplant.

Julie and I have encouraged Zander and Riley to compete every year since they were young. They both completed their first ten-kilometer walk-run at the ages of nine and seven and have competed almost every year since then with Julie and me.

But six miles on a horizontal plane is not the same as six miles of steep climbing.

## Fourteeners

I had not yet climbed one of the famed fourteeners, mountaineering slang for a mountain that meets or exceeds 14,000 feet[20] above sea level. In the United Kingdom, Ben Nevis is the highest peak at 4,413 feet[21], less than a third of the height of a Colorado fourteener (overseas visitors are often astonished to learn that they are already higher than the highest mountain in Britain simply by arriving at Denver International Airport). To remedy the oversight, I determinedly joined a squad of high school rowers and escorting adults in July 2014 to summit my first fourteener, Mount Bierstadt. I was accompanied by my friend, Jean Cornec.

Jean is a Frenchman from Brittany. With dry Gallic humor, he does not pass up an opportunity to point out that he is actually not French, but *Breton*. As a geologist, he is used to being outdoors and navigating inhospitable terrain. He applies his geological skills to his second *de facto* occupation of explorer. He has literally spent years wandering in remote jungles of Central and South America prospecting for oil and precious metals. When you ask Jean how he is, he replies, "Fine. I found a gold mine." And he's not kidding. This morning, he was fascinated by the intricacies of the surrounding rock structures as we climbed.

The awe-inspiring presence of a fourteener is hard to overstate. I marveled at the sheer size and scale of the mountain. There are ninety-six fourteeners in the United Sates, fifty-three of

---

20  4,270m
21  1,345m

which are in Colorado. Mount Bierstadt (named after a landscape painter who climbed it in the 1860s) stands at 14,060[22] feet and has the distinction of being a relatively straightforward ascent. Its better-known neighbor, Mount Evans, has a road up to the summit if you feel like a mountain adventure without exertion. As Mount Bierstadt is only sixty miles from metro Denver, it is readily accessible to weekend adventurers. At 6:45 a.m. on a Saturday in July, the first challenge was finding a roadside parking spot.

I was especially interested to find out how my breathing would function at altitude. As we started the climb and quickly rose above the tree-line at about twelve thousand feet, I started to notice the air's thinness. I was breathing slowly, cautiously, and walking at a measured pace. Rising through thirteen thousand feet, my breaths became shorter and shallower. But I noticed, with quiet satisfaction, so were Jean's. Other hikers were less garrulous than they were at the trail head, as they opted to save their breath for the climb. Some had more labored breathing than others. I'm usually not one for gloating, but I allowed myself a moment of *schadenfreude* at some of the more audible panting. I'm pretty sure they all had their original lungs. Head down, I kept going.

The trail was marked by a series of cairns, but we didn't need much guidance as visibility was perfect and the air temperature was warm. After about three hours of walking, with only a couple of water breaks, we had gained over three thousand feet and covered three miles. Once we navigated an extensive boulder field, we reached the summit.

The view was phenomenal. It was a crystal-clear day and we could see for twenty miles out across the interlinked tangle of mountain peaks in a wonderous three-hundred-and-sixty-degree panorama. I could detect a mild feeling of dizziness, as my lungs worked to absorb fragments of oxygen from the thin air.

A lighting strike may sound implausible but is a perennial danger to exposed hikers on an open mountain. Storms are more

---

22   4,267m

likely in June, July and August, and later in the day, hence the
early start and descent before lunch. In the previous ten years,
seventeen people were killed by lightning strikes in Colorado
alone[23]. After all I have been through, I thought, I'll be darned
if I am going to be taken out at this point by a lightning bolt
– although perhaps there would be a small degree of poetic
justice for my latent agnosticism. Jean is taller than me. I assured
him that his suspicion that I only brought him along to act as
a lightning rod was completely unfounded. Nevertheless, we
stayed on the summit for only twenty minutes before starting
the descent.

The way down was much faster than the ascent and we were
back at the parking area before noon. The air at the somewhat
derisory altitude of eleven thousand feet felt positively woolly
with oxygen. My legs were tired, and my feet were sore inside
my boots, but my breathing was clear and - dare I say it - normal.

---

23 From 2005-2014, Colorado had the third-most lightning-strike
fatalities of any state, with 17. Another 15 were injured, according to
the National Weather Service. Florida is by far the most dangerous
state for lightning, averaging more than 10 deaths per year. Source:
www.coloradoan.com 5/14/15

Zander and Gavin on Grays Peak summit in Colorado (14,270 ft).
August 2014 (photo: Jean Cornec)

Riley & Gavin at Boston Harbor finish.
September 2014

# CHAPTER EIGHT: BRIDGE-TO-BRIDGE

*We don't belong in the sea. The sea is full of things that bite us, sting us, hurt the soles of our feet, and it's extremely cold. When are we gonna take the hint that the things that live in the sea don't like us?*

- Billy Connolly

**Seven years post-transplant:**
**a six-mile swim starting at zero dark thirty**

It is still quite dark at Fisherman's Wharf at 4:30 a.m., even in mid-summer. The taxi had just pulled up at the quay side. Zander, Riley, Julie and I piled out. The sea breeze was light and we could immediately smell the salty air. It was Saturday morning, August 8th, 2015.

"You're doing what?" The taxi driver eyed us skeptically as he picked us up at the hotel. At this hour, he was more accustomed to ferrying bleary-eyed party goers home than picking up a wetsuit-clad family clearly bordering on insanity.

"It's called the bridge-to-bridge swim," Riley piped up, as if the term was in common usage. "We are going to swim from the Golden Gate Bridge to the Bay Bridge."

The taxi driver raised his eyebrows but didn't reply.

"It's six-point-two miles," Riley added helpfully. Still no response. We rode the rest of the short journey in silence.

At the near-deserted wharf, we saw a small group of people standing at the quayside in long swim jackets and woolen hats: swim buddies, who else?

The group included our swim master, Warren Wallace, with whom I had exchanged emails. Warren was in his early thirties, relaxed and smiling, in a warm hat and fleece jacket. As the founder of Odyssey Open Water Swimming, a group that organizes swims in and around San Francisco, he was an experienced open-water swimmer himself. After introductions to the other early morning swimmers, he pointed to the boat tied to the quay-side.

"The captain will be here shortly," he said. "Then we'll get going. We'll meet the kayakers out by the bridge. Jump time is five-thirty."

"Oh, another thing," he said, looking almost apologetic as if he had forgotten a detail. "I'll hand out your lights once we get out there."

Lights? What lights? I half-smiled and looked at Zander and Riley quizzically. Did they know what he was talking about? They both shrugged and shook their heads. The sun would be up soon. Who would need lights?

I soon found out.

The boat's captain arrived, a heavily-set bearded salty dog skipper, and we all boarded the vessel. I counted eleven swimmers. In addition to Warren and Julie, our friends, Wanda Hellevang and her daughter, Aysha, who had travelled from Calgary, joined us for this adventure. Wanda and I were friends from our studies at business school in the 1990s.

The ropes were cast off, the boat went hard astern, turned around, and powered out of the harbor. Next stop was the iconic Golden Gate Bridge. It was exactly 5:00 a.m.

To the west, we could see the feeble lights that partly illuminated the massive towers of the red-tinged Golden Gate Bridge. To the east, the lesser known, but much better lit, four-mile-long Oakland Bay Bridge (the Bay Bridge) silently connected San Francisco to Oakland, via Yerba Buena Island. It stood majestic and aloof. That was our challenge this dark morning: to swim the six miles from one bridge to the other.

It is hard to overstate the hugeness of the Golden Gate Bridge. Opened in 1937, it features heavily in popular culture as one of the most recognizable symbols of the United States. We have all seen it from the safety of the shore, from one of its six toll lanes, or as a movie opening sequence (Wikipedia lists over seventy movies in which the bridge is featured). In the blackness and eeriness, we were going to be right underneath it.

The boat ploughed doggedly towards the gargantuan structure through a surprisingly heavy swell. Everyone was excited. The swimmers were talking animatedly. All of us wore thermal swim jackets and hats to avoid getting cold. There would be enough cold to go around once we got in the water.

Julie and Wanda clung to the boat's rails, mesmerized by the approaching bridge. Wanda in turn clung to Aysha. Eight-year-old Aysha's eyes were wide as saucers she absorbed her surroundings. I am not sure what Wanda had told her what to expect of her trip to the United States, but I'm sure this was not it.

As we neared the bridge, Warren started handing out lights. Yes, lights. Small, golf ball-sized luminous green lights with a little clip.

"Attach these to the back of your head on your goggle strap," he told us cheerfully. "The light will help the kayakers know where you are."

Know where you are! I could see the expression on Julie's face. She would tell later of her total alarm at the prospect of her whole family jumping over the side into an abyss of blackness.

The early start was designed to avoid other water craft - speed boats, jet skis, and fishing boats – which assembled on the bay on any given Saturday morning. Julie assumed – as I had - that it would be daylight when we started to swim.

Not so. We had passed Alcatraz Island on the way out to the bridge, but we only knew it because of the faint dot of a pulsing red light atop an antenna on one of the crumbling buildings. And yes, Alcatraz is even more eerie than usual in the dark.

## "Swim towards Alcatraz, then turn right"

The engines eased as we neared the center of the giant pillars beneath the bridge. The boat surged up and down in the swell without its forward momentum. In my mind, old mountaineer's adage of "don't look down!" could aptly be inverted. Someone could easily have told me, "don't look up!" and I would have known what they meant. But look up I did.

The rust-colored bridge hung two hundred feet above us like an ominous giant. It was a similar feeling of size and insignificance to walking into one of those massive European Gothic cathedrals and staring with neck-bending wonder at the ceiling. The enormous bridge pillars stood to the left and to the right. In between and to the west, I thought to myself, the next stop was the Pacific. To the east, the lights twinkled from the Bay Bridge and the city of San Francisco. Horror gripped my stomach. Are we really going to do this?

Warren was shouting. My mind jolted back to the task at hand. The detailed briefing was about to start. Everyone was suddenly attentive.

"Look over there," he yelled to be heard above the sound of the boat's idling engines and pointed eastward into the blackness. "That's Alcatraz. Swim towards Alcatraz, then turn right." He paused for a moment. "Okay, that's it. Jump time!"

That's it? That was the briefing? What about the tides, the currents? What about the weather? Where is my kayaker? What is the water temperature? That was the briefing? I felt a renewed surge of panic.

"Oh, and another thing," Warren continued.

There's more. I felt relieved. At least we were going to get some further words of wisdom to help with the challenge ahead.

"Don't stop swimming until you get to the bridge. As long as you have forward motion, we won't pull you out. Just keep going!" He swung his arms to indicate the boat's stern.

"Jump time!"

Everyone crowded together and started discarding jackets and hats. That really was the end of the briefing. Most of us were already wetsuited and at least two intrepid characters in our group were only wearing swimsuits. Swimming purists, as they would undoubtedly regard themselves, despite the frigid sixty-one degree[24] water. Anyone who tells you that the Pacific Ocean in Northern California is warm enough for enjoyable bare skin swimming is a self-avowed masochist.

The implausibly small green lights were suddenly everywhere, as each swimmer clipped a little light onto their goggle straps. Splash! Splash! The first two swimmers went over the side.

---

24   16°C

Wait, are we going now? Where the hell are our kayakers? I looked around anxiously for Zander and Riley. They were both swim-capped and lowering their goggles, standing behind the next swimmer who was about to jump. Julie gave them both kisses and stood back. Both kids were smiling and seemed relaxed. It was not how I felt at all. I tried to suppress feelings of abject panic.

Unseen by me, Warren had pre-arranged a dozen kayakers to support the swimmers and they had arrived on scene, having launched from the city side of the bridge. They jostled around the boat now, barely visible in the boat's dim lights, chatting and laughing like noisy seals in the surging water.

Splash, splash, splash! Three more swimmers vanished over the side. Splash, splash, splash! Three more went in. I could see the tiny green lights as they bobbed for a moment beside the boat, then slowly started fanning out to the east as the swim started.

Then was just three of us left standing on the stern, looking down into the water. My stomach was in knots. I was petrified. Oh my gosh, I don't think I can do this, I suddenly realized.

"Find a kayaker and stick with him," Warren yelled, pointing over the side.

Without further hesitation, Zander stepped up onto the railing and jumped. Riley was right behind him. Both hit the water, pow, pow. They submerged briefly, popped to the surface, and started to swim. Their two little green lights were all I could see of them.

I was the last swimmer still on the boat. I looked down at the water. Black. Cold. I could not turn back now. The kids were already in there. I had to jump. I swallowed hard. No choice. Have to go. Jump, you coward, jump.

I took a deep breath, closed my eyes, and stepped forward into the darkness.

## Patchy prep

This adventure had been months in the planning. Over two years before, Zander, Riley and I had completed the Alcatraz swim. As part of the post-swim chatter from that event, we overheard other swimmers talking about the "bridge-to-bridge" swim as a logical progression. It was a longer swim, six miles compared to just over one mile, but in the same waters and with the same spectacular views of San Francisco.

At the time of completing that swim, I remember recovering on a grassy bank, sipping hot tea, and trying to control my chattering teeth. As I looked out across the bay, the Golden Gate Bridge was to my left, and the Bay Bridge was to my right. I remember thinking how far apart the bridges seemed, and how much cold water lay in between them. But you know, maybe one day. Maybe.

Regardless of what I thought, the seed had been irretrievably planted in my daughter's imagination. When we completed the Alcatraz swim, Zander was thirteen and Riley was eleven years old and, at the time, it was one of the most exciting physical accomplishments of their young lives. They had received a lot of positive feedback from family and friends, as well as being interviewed by a BBC journalist, with the interview video and story posted on the BBC's website.

Both kids had continued to develop physically and athletically since then and by August of 2015 were sixteen and fourteen-years-old. Riley and I had completed the Boston harbor swim in the fall of 2014. Zander had crew rowing commitments which had largely replaced swimming for him. What was not obvious to me was obvious to them. The summer was the perfect time for another big swim.

The prospect of a swim expedition with Zander and Riley also gave me the opportunity to plan a fundraising drive around the event to support post-lung transplant research. From various discussions with my pulmonologist, Scott Palmer, MD, I was aware how much he and his team of researchers relied upon independent financial help to support his on-going work at Duke University. A big swim like this one would give us an event around which to generate awareness, interest and funds.

An online search quickly established that we could register for the bridge-to-bridge swim later in the summer of 2015. I found Odyssey's website and looked in awe at the inspiring photos of smiling people in wetsuits. Later, I corresponded with Warren, and established the parameters of a possible swim. It was time to commit to a date.

"Hey, Riley. Are you up for bridge-to-bridge this summer?" I asked casually one afternoon. She immediately knew exactly what I meant.

"Yes."

"Are you sure?"

"Dad, yes." There was no doubt in her voice.

"Will you train?"

"Yes, of course. I will join swim the team at Rally Sport for the summer and train with them in the evenings. They are hard core!"

"What about Zander?"

"He'll do it." Again, there was no doubt in her voice.

Later that evening, Zander was in the kitchen. "Want to swim bridge-to-bridge with Riley and I later this summer?" I prodded.

"Sure." He sounded hesitant.

"Are you okay? Are you certain you want to do it?" I asked.

"Well, yes."

"You don't have to do it. Don't do it just because Riley is doing it," I said, knowing the mental benchmark he would use. "Only do it if you really want to."

"Yes, I'll do it. But there's one thing." He sounded uncomfortable.

"What?"

"I don't want to train for it."

"What do you mean you don't want to train for it? How are going to swim six miles without training? That's not going to work." I felt exasperated.

"I will keep rowing. I will run. I just don't enjoy swimming up and down in a pool. It's boring."

Perhaps he had a point. While I always found swimming to be the most relaxing and energizing way of exercising, I could still appreciate that it was not for everyone. Zander was a competitive rower on a junior crew team in Colorado and had competed the last summer at the Youth National Championships. He knew how to train and push himself physically and mentally.

Additionally, rowing is one of those wonderful full-body exercises - like swimming and cross-country skiing - where literally every muscle in your body gets a thorough work out. He would probably manage the swim if he committed to daily rowing and running. Besides, apart from him being a natural swimmer, he was sixteen. He had the benefit of exuberant youth on his side.

I conceded, with one condition. There was a competitive three-mile lake swim coming up in July. It was one of several organized open-water swims in Colorado over the summer – together known as the Mountain Swim Series – notwithstanding that landlocked Colorado is a somewhat unlikely venue for open-water swimming. My condition was that he had to swim the three-mile swim in Carter Lake, near Berthoud, Colorado, with me, to qualify for the San Francisco swim.

"Deal?" I offered.

He readily agreed. "Deal!"

Training with the masters group at Colorado Athletic Club in Boulder four or five times a week was already my normal routine. A *masters* program usually does not necessarily allude to mastering anything. The annual Masters Tournament in Augusta, Georgia, is the exception, where a certain mastery of golf is probably a prerequisite. The term *masters* was originally applied to adults who competed in track and field athletics and, in swimming, simply means participants above eighteen years old. The bulk of masters swimmers are generally in the thirty to sixty-year-old range, but there is no upper age limit. The US Masters Swimming website currently lists competitors in the categories of Men's 90-94 years old and Women's 95-99 years old.

In a seventy-five-minute pool session, the slower lane swimmers routinely chalk up 3,000 meters, while the faster lane swimmers easily top 4,000 meters, all under the aegis of a pool-side coach. With five Monday to Saturday sessions, even a slow-lane swimmer could tuck a weekly diet of 15,000 meters under his or her aquatic belt.

Swim training does not have to be mind-numbingly boring. On the contrary, a session in a swim lane comprised of up to seven evenly-matched athletes who bash out sets of coach-directed activity requires a lot of focused concentration.

Sessions are built up with sets of warm-up laps, drills, combinations of arms only, legs only, back, front, interval sets, and cool downs. They test mental agility as much as physical fitness. Wily coaches keep the combinations moving and rest intervals short, so that the sessions pass in no time.

There is significant evidence that exercising with others improves performance and motivation. I am aware of athletes who have the self-discipline to train on their own, but I am not one of them. I have always found that I get energy from others, as well as the motivation to keep going when I get tired, even if only from a feeling of not wanting others see me give up. I am the first to admit that without the camaraderie of my lane mates, and the supervision of an artful coach, my motivation quickly evaporates.

The three-mile Carter Lake swim in July 2015 was a success. Riley was unfortunately ineligible to swim as the lower age limit for the event was sixteen. Zander and I started along with over a hundred early risers at one end of the freshwater lake and swam all the way to the other end, three miles away. Julie was on the water in a support kayak.

Zander wore my wetsuit as he had outgrown his own one. I opted to swim without one. The water was calm and bearably cold. Fresh water is certainly a more challenging swim than salt water as it is significantly less buoyant. A wetsuit will make up for that loss of buoyancy as it lets a swimmer lie higher in the water, which results in more speed. A wetsuited swimmer probably swims around ten percent faster than a comparable bare-skin swimmer.

Zander completed the swim in a heroic one hour, twenty-nine minutes. I came in a slightly less heroic one hour and fifty-two minutes, placing fifteenth out of sixteen competitors in the men's 40-49 years age group (thereby achieving my universal goal of not being in last place). Zander felt tired at the end, as did I, but mission accomplished. Zander could bask in the glory of having cleared our self-imposed bar to qualify for the Big Swim the following month.

## Acclimatization

To prep for the frigid waters of the North Pacific, Riley and I decided to acclimatize with an experimental series of ice baths. A trip to the supermarket and five bags of ice later, we ran a bath and poured ice into the already cold water.

Our target was submersion up to the neck for twenty minutes. We set a timer and put on some loud pop music. I went first. Once your body gets over the initial shock of pins and needles, it begins to settle into the cold. Strangely, I found the cold water strangely relaxing and calming, although the feeling of cold never really went away.

There are a lot of studies that show that repeated exposure to cold will result in increased cold tolerance. Such acclimation usually takes the form of daily cold baths or showers that don't even have to be all that cold (water is good at conducting heat away from the skin): sixty-eight degrees[25] will get the job done.

Captain Robert Scott's name is inseparably associated with Antarctic exploration. He probably knew a thing or two about cold. One of his crew members, "Birdie" (H.R.) Bowers, was notable for his extreme hardiness. Scott described how he had "never seen anyone so unaffected by cold." Bowers was able to sleep soundly in conditions where others were unable to sleep because of extreme shivering. Bowers' toughness can probably be attributed to a regime of stripping naked and throwing buckets of icy water over himself every morning in the Antarctic, not something that would suit everyone.

Once my twenty minutes were up, I swapped places with Riley, and added some more ice. Not to be outdone by her Dad, Riley determinedly stuck it out until she reached her own target time: twenty minutes and five seconds.

The ice baths were an interesting experiment, but I'm not convinced that they helped very much, as we did not take them

---

25  20°C

regularly enough. Besides, as Riley pointed out, Captain Scott and all his crew froze to death in the Antarctic. Maybe not such a great example after all.

## Aquatic bliss

I loved the silkiness of the water on my face as I swam away from the boat. Most swimmers have a naturally favored breathing side, either left or right. The optimal way to balance is to breathe bilaterally, alternating left and right side, with every third arm stroke. As I swam in the cold, my breathing self-discipline deserted me, and I automatically defaulted to my left side on each stroke cycle to get enough air. All my nervousness in jumping into the darkness had gone. I felt much more at home in the water and swam forward.

I had been working on sighting, which involved lifting your head clear of the water on each fourth stroke cycle to get a visual fix on a stationary landmark. It allows a swimmer to avoid zig-zagging which can add unwelcome distance to a swim. Being right-handed and being used to following markings on a pool floor, I swim with a left bias if I do not correct my stroke. All I could do was snatch a glimpse of the tiny red light on the dark shadow that was Alcatraz Island as my head came up to sight.

My kayaker was never more than a few yards away. With a swim cap and the noise of the water, it was impossible to hear clearly, but occasionally I would pause to look around, and he would give a few words of encouragement. I was aware of the water's coldness, but it was not inhibitive.

But the swell was powerful, and I could feel the drift of the current. The swim was tide-assisted, meaning that you go with the incoming tide. The occasional cormorant, darting along just inches above the surface of the water, was startled by my presence and would swerve to avoid a collision.

Many people ask about sharks in open-water swimming. One source[26] lists eleven species of shark in the San Francisco Bay. The most common are leopard sharks and the bottom-feeding

---

26   www.sfbaywildlife.info/species/sharks (accessed 11/10/2017)

spiny dogfish, neither of which are dangerous to humans. Of course, the predator that everyone wants to ask about is the great white shark.

While there have been no recorded shark attacks on swimmers in the bay, there have been several great white shark sightings. The conventional wisdom, we believed, was that great white sharks may be in the vicinity but generally do not venture beyond the Golden Gate Bridge. But I was too focused on my breath and swimming on the surface to think of anything that might be lurking below.

I knew that the other swimmers were in front of me. Through the oscillating waves, I could occasionally catch a glimpse of another yellow swim cap in the distance before it vanished again.

I was adjacent to Alcatraz by now and my kayaker called over to tell me to pivot a sixty-degree angle to the right to start swimming towards the city. "Sight off the Transamerica Pyramid building," he yelled. The eight hundred and fifty feet pin-like tower was an easily-sighted target on the city skyline. I kept it in front of me as I moved steadily through the cold water, all the while being pushed towards the Bay Bridge.

The swell had flattened out and it was easier to maintain a consistent stroke. I was pleased that my breathing felt deep and strong. At the start of any exertion, I always feel out of breath until my lungs open and allow me to breathe properly. By this point in the swim, I was taking wonderfully deep breaths, which made me feel positive and strong. I knew I was going to complete the swim. With expeditions like this, you are never one hundred percent sure at the outset that you will finish. There is always the unexpected; a negative reaction to the cold, a muscle cramp, weather, or just a bad swim day.

But all was well today. I felt calm, focused, and mentally settled into enjoy the serenity of the remainder of the swim.

I could see the orange flag of a kayaker ahead, which meant that there was a swimmer with him. As I got closer, I could see that he was barely moving, swimming with slow deliberate strokes. It was difficult to identify him, as we all wore yellow swim caps, goggles, and black wetsuits.

I pushed forward and gradually gained on the lagging swimmer. Within ten minutes, I reached him. I would recognize that silhouette anywhere. Zander! As I caught him, I touched his foot

"Hey, Zan," I gasped. "How're you feeling?"

"Tired." He looked discouraged.

"Not far to go," I urged. "Probably about a mile." I nodded towards the Bay Bridge in the distance.

I think Zander was surprised to see me alongside him, and suddenly got a renewed burst of energy to push him on. For a sixteen-year-old, the idea of being outswam by his old man was mortifying. He picked up his stroke cadence and churned on. Initially, I tried to keep up and swim alongside him, but he was too strong, and steadily moved ahead.

The Bay Bridge was dead ahead. The structure that had seemed so small in the distance was now towering above me. The support boat with the other swimmers, Julie, Wanda, and Aysha, was floating in the calm water. I swam alongside the boat, grabbed on to the ladder that was hanging down, and laboriously hauled myself up and onto the deck. I was the last of the eleven swimmers to finish.

"Hey, Dad!" Riley and Zander were there, as were Julie, Aysha and Wanda. Despite feeling tired and cold, I felt a tremendous surge of accomplishment. Ten kilometers, bridge-to-bridge. I had done it!

On deck, I started to peel off my wetsuit while Julie updated me. Riley had reached the boat in just over two-and-a half hours. In her typical matter-of-fact fashion, she had swum strongly and fearlessly until she reached the boat. Here she was, wrapped in a towel, relaxed, chatting and smiling. The swim was not really a competitive event but to Riley everything is a competition.

"I came in fourth!" she exclaimed gleefully.

Zander came in fifteen minutes after Riley. He was quiet, having stripped off his wetsuit, and was warming up. Although he would not admit it, I think he realized that the concept of not swim training for an open-water swim was not the smartest thing in the world. Oh well, live and learn.

Julie filled me in on her experience. Not one to be intimidated lightly, she had found the role of tireless supporter rather harrowing that day.

---

"I was scared from the moment we arrived at the dock and boarded the boat," Julie recounted later. Her experience on the support boat did not exactly match our serene view from the water.

"It was so dark. I did not think it could not get any darker. Once the boat left the harbor, it was pitch black. All I could think about was the spinning light on Alcatraz and how scary it was. As the boat pulled closer to the Golden Gate Bridge and the swimmers became more excited, I just became more scared."

"The bridge looked like something out of a Transformers movie. Was my family really going to jump overboard into the blackness? The support kayakers were low in the water, so were barely visible."

"When the swim master pulled out those stupid little lights, no bigger than a quarter, and told the swimmers to snap them onto their goggles, I almost had a fit. Those little lights? They were like the toys you find in a cereal box. That's how we were going to keep track of my family in the water? I wanted to throw up."

"Once the boat was in place beneath the bridge, Zander was the first over the side with only the briefest hesitation. Riley followed with no hesitation. Gavin did hesitate. He stood on the stern, looking down into the water for several seconds. He was the last swimmer still on the boat. I have seen a similar look on this face only once before; it was definitely fear. Then he too jumped.

"Wanda, Aysha and I watched in silence as the tiny green lights fanned out in the black water. I could not tell who was who. All the lights looked the same. And they all spread out quickly. Any advice that had been given to the swimmers about staying together in the water was totally disregarded."

"The boat bobbed for quite some time beneath the bridge, giving the swimmers time to make some headway. Not even one of those stupid little lights were visible any longer. All I could see was darkness. I told myself it will be so much better once it got lighter.

"On the contrary, daybreak brought a new and totally unexpected peril: pleasure boats. As the darkness receded, watercraft began emerging from the Oakland side of the bay. The captain of our support boat had already informed us that he had followed the letter of the law in notifying the Coast Guard of the swim, as well as flying the requisite maritime flag from his mast to let other watercraft know that there were swimmers in the water. Despite each swimmer having an accompanying kayaker, the biggest danger was not from drowning or from nefarious sea creatures, but from other boats. Two or three fishing vessels initially drew close but took a wide berth when they recognized the warning flag.

"Trouble arose when recreational power boats came surging across the bay, blind and ignorant to any potential hazards in the water. On two separate occasions, these speed boats were whipping over the water and coming perilously close to the swimmers."

"Both times, the captain veered our vessel to act as a shield between the swimmers and the power boats. But it was a fishing boat, so the maneuver was painfully slow. Additionally, a friend of one of the swimmers was separately following the progression of the swim in his own small boat. He also deftly steered his boat between the swimmers and power boats as an additional barrier, no easy task given the spread of the swimmers."

"The power boats made me terrified. Hearts pumping, Wanda, Warren and I scrambled to the highest point of the boat, desperately waving our arms and yelling like crazy people. STOP! LOOK OUT! SWIMMERS IN THE WATER!

"Our boat's captain was apoplectic. He sounded blast after blast on the ship's horn and screamed a stream of expletive-laden invective at the power boats. He used every curse word in the book - and probably a few more - as he swore at the reckless boaters like, well, a sailor."

"Finally seeing a boat, if not swimmers, in their path, the power boats were forced to reduce speed and change course, thereby narrowly missing our swimmers. One of them had the nerve to slow his boat and return a slew of verbal abuse at us. He did not have his radio turned on, so could not hear our warnings. He was oblivious to any Coast Guard reports, clueless about our boat's warning flag, and the danger he posed to the kayakers and swimmers."

"We were all furious about the threats posed by the irresponsible boaters. This extra anxiety was not at all what I had bargained for. These aggressive encounters abruptly turned an otherwise calm cruise into a high-stress situation. I must have aged ten years that morning."

"Our support boat eventually reached the Oakland Bridge, the engine idling as we waited for the swimmers beneath the giant grey towers. I remember seeing the first three swimmers reach the boat and pull themselves up the ladder. I strained my eyes expectantly to see if my children and husband were among the incoming yellow dots of swim caps. Suddenly, a swimmer was coming up the ladder. Her goggled face was almost unrecognizable, caked in foamy slime. She was smiling broadly. It was Riley!

"Twenty minutes later, Zander arrived, exhausted. "I'm never doing that again," he spluttered.

"A few minutes later, the last swimmer of the group, Gavin, also smiling, pulled himself up the ladder and onto the deck.

"Everyone was safe and sound. I have never felt so relived in my life."

---

After catching our breath over a hot breakfast of sugared coffee, toast, and eggs, our group of six decided to take in the tourist sights of the city. The best way seemed to be on an organized tour using bright yellow amphibious vehicles known as the Duck Tour.

Once the tour got underway, the driver-guide, the self-proclaimed, and undoubtedly self-appointed, Captain Mike, kept up an uproarious rapid-fire commentary over the loud speaker on all things San Francisco. He delivered a wealth of facts and figures as we passed though streets and a waterway, and as well as delivering a stream of well-trodden jokes such as "Lombard Street, well-known as the second crookedest street in the world… the first being Wall Street!" The banter was accompanied by pumping seventies hits like Village People's *YMCA*. You get the idea. The passengers loved it.

As the Golden Gate Bridge and Alcatraz Island came into view, Captain Mike explained that the San Francisco Bay is an estuary. Fresh water flows down from the Sacramento and San Joaquin rivers, as well as the Sierra Nevada mountains, and meets the incoming salt water from the Pacific Ocean.

One of the many interesting facts about this melding of the waters, he went on with a villainous smirk, was about great white sharks. When these awesome predators swim under the Golden Gate Bridge into the bay, they can only swim as far as Alcatraz. They are forced to turn back as they are unable to maintain their salt water buoyancy in the predominantly fresh water from the mountains.

Notably, he used the words *when* the great white sharks swim into the bay, not *if* they swim into the bay. As someone who took an obvious pride in his knowledge, Captain Mike clearly savored his audience's reactions to his shark stories.

Zander and Riley were sitting together in the seat row in front of me up until then, enjoying the entertainment. Captain Mike's words were not lost on them. They turned around simultaneously to look at me, eyes wide.

"Great whites?

"As far as Alcatraz?"

"Dad…!"

Tiny lights of bridge-to-bridge swimmers.
August 2015 (photo: Wanda Hellevang)

"Swim towards Alcatraz, then turn right."
August 2015.

Bridge-to-bridge finish August 2015.
Left-to-right (back): Gavin, Zander, Warren Wallace;
(front) Riley (photo: Julie)

Riley & Julie after bridge-to-bridge swim.
August 2015

# CHAPTER NINE: DON'T TAKE YOUR ORGANS TO HEAVEN

*"Don't take your organs to heaven with you. Heaven knows we need them here."*

- Unknown

## Gift of life

Organ transplant is the selfless gift of a living, breathing body part. It is given without the expectation of anything in return. It is a gift of such immensity and value that nothing could be regarded as adequate compensation. It is literally the "gift of life."

I did not have any information about my lung donor. The lungs had been helicoptered to Duke, but that fact alone did not tell me very much. My donor likely came from the eastern seaboard of the United States. I also knew from reading about transplant medicine that I would be approximately the same physical size as my donor - five feet, nine inches tall - and would have the same blood type of A+[27].

I often wondered about my lung donor. The family must have experienced such pain. The transplant was one of the best days in my life when I received the gift of life. The corollary would be one of the worst days for my donor family.

I have heard that organ transplant recipients often feel a sense of guilt when they receive a deceased person's organs. I felt many emotions during the drawn-out process of transplant - raw fear, trepidation, anxiety, elation - but guilt was not one of them. To me, the death of my donor was entirely independent of my need for new lungs.

What I really wanted to know was whether my donor was male or female, his or her age, where he or she lived, what he or

---

27  An A+ blood type can receive blood form A+ and O+ blood type donors, which together make up over seventy percent of the population.

she did, what his or her personality was like? In short, I wanted to know all the information to get to know someone.

"You should write a thank you letter to your donor family," advised my post-transplant coordinator just before being discharged from hospital. "You might not get a reply, but it's the right thing to do."

She was right. It was the right thing to do. A mere thank you letter seemed inadequate given the magnitude of what I had received. But then again, I could not think of any other way to reach out.

In the United States, the "HIPAA" legislation (the Health Insurance Portability and Accountability Act) requires, among other things, the protection and confidential handling of patient data. For a transplant recipient, the practical result is that no information about a donor can be released without permission from the donor's family. The hospital team probably had limited knowledge of the donor anyway, but they were still appropriately tight-lipped.

**Thank you**

Julie, Zander, Riley, and I decided to write the first of what turned into several thank you cards and letters to the donor family within weeks of my operation. We sent them to my hospital with a request to pass them along to the donor family.

It was difficult to know what to write. I merely wrote "thank you" and briefly explained that I had received new lungs and was doing well. Zander was nine and Riley was seven by then, so both could express themselves adequately.

"Thank you for saving my Dad," Zander wrote simply, and signed his name.

"Thank you, from Riley xxx," wrote Riley on her own pink sheet of paper and enclosed a drawing. Julie also included a note and we put the pieces of paper into an envelope and sent them off.

Weeks passed and no reply. I knew that it was the donor family's choice whether to reply or not, but I hoped that I would hear from them. At the same time, Julie and I recognized that it was entirely possible that we would never receive a response, as is the case for most transplant recipients, I understood.

In my post-transplant life, I am in regular contact with a transplant coordinator at Duke for maintenance, such as monthly blood work evaluations, appointment scheduling and, of course, prescription refills. About a year post-transplant, I asked my transplant coordinator if she could provide any non-identifying information about my donor. I was hoping to learn at least if the donor was male or female and his or her age.

"I'm sorry, Gavin, it's not possible," she wrote back by email. "It would involve going to the medical archives and looking up the information. With my volume of regular patients, I just don't have time. I hope you understand."

Yes, I understood. It was still frustrating.

Over time, I met many people who were touched by organ transplant. At a fundraising event organized by the American Transplant Foundation in Denver, I talked to a volunteer who introduced herself as an organ donor mother. In the unearthly world of transplant, you get used to a certain proximity to death. Most cases of organ transplant – except for directed and altruistic kidney and some partial-liver donations – invariably mean that someone has died to make the donation possible. By introducing herself as the mother of a donor, it was understood that she had lost a child. Apart from saying "sorry for your loss" it is difficult to come up with anything else, especially when you have just met someone. In this case, she was quite forthcoming. Perhaps it helped her to speak openly about her loss.

She told me that she had received several letters from the recipients of her son's organs. She had even met some of them. If you write to the donor family, they do get your letters, she assured me. It may just be emotionally difficult for them to make contact, given the trauma, but it was only through letters that you had any hope of reaching them.

"Sometimes it takes months, even years, before they write back to you," she told me. "But they often do. In my case, it helped my family and me reach closure by knowing that someone benefitted from my son's death."

The first year's anniversary of my transplant arrived. It was a big event for us. It would also be a significant anniversary for my donor's family: one year since the death of their loved one. I decided to write another letter to them.

---

March 9th, 2009

Dear Donor Family,

I wanted to write you another letter as we approach the first anniversary of the passing of your loved one. I received lungs on March 14th, 2008.

I am very conscious that without your kind agreement to donate the organ, I would not be writing to you today. Your donation has allowed me to get the lung transplant that I needed to save my life. I have been able to spend the last 12 months in better and better health with my wife and young family (Julie, Zander, aged 9, and Riley, aged 7).

It is difficult to adequately express my gratitude at receiving the lungs. I understand that it has meant heartbreak for you. I can only hope that you may feel some sense of purpose through knowing that your loss, and your loved one's organs, have done so much to benefit other people.

It would mean a lot if you feel able to get in touch. I would like to express my gratitude to you. If you would like to make contact, please get in touch with your hospital, and they will contact me via my hospital. I hope you feel able to do this.

Sincerely,
Gavin Maitland

---

Months, then years passed, and still no response. I began to accept that I might never know from whom I had received my beautiful, precious lungs.

I often contemplated whether I was any different with my new lungs. Beyond the physiological fit, there is no other known transfer with an organ transplant, meaning that no characteristics of an organ donor's personality are transferred to the recipient. That may seem intuitive, but several people have asked me post-transplant whether there was any cross over. If my donor had liked strawberry ice-cream, for example, would I now have a proclivity for strawberry ice cream?

Lungs are generally not associated with emotion in the same way as the heart. Expressions like "have a heart" or to "take heart" are synonymous with courage, generosity and, ultimately, humanity. In Scotland, a lot of significance is attached to the heart of Robert the Bruce, the original Braveheart. The shriveled relic was re-discovered during an archeological dig in Scotland in 1996 and is widely believed to be the actual heart of the magnanimous fourteenth century warrior king. Whether any of the emotion attributed to the heart itself remains is doubtful, but the symbolism is powerful.

Unlike the hopes of the Cowardly Lion or the Tinman in the 1939 classic *The Wizard of Oz*, courage and feelings are not transferred with a heart transplant, despite the emotive symbolism. Neither did my new lungs give me any hitherto unknown cravings or hankerings.

I resigned myself to the fact that perhaps I would never hear from the donor family. Perhaps the letters were not being passed on. Perhaps my lungs had come from an elderly person with no relatives. Perhaps no one was receiving the letters. Perhaps there was, in fact, no "donor family."

Then, one morning in 2011, almost three years after my lung transplant, I got a response. I arrived at my office, opened my computer, and immediately saw an email from Carolina Donor Services. I knew exactly what it was. It said that the donor family had consented to release their contact information. The letter also counseled that I should consider carefully whether I wanted to make contact. It may be an emotional experience on both sides and, once made, the contact could not be undone. Legal release forms were attached to the email.

I did not have to consider the decision for more than a millisecond. I printed out the forms, signed, scanned, and emailed them back.

For the next week or so, nothing happened. I knew this was not a fast process. I was not thinking about it. My mobile phone rang. My mind was wrapped around the intricacies of a work spreadsheet problem and I did not recognize the caller-ID number. I answered absent-mindedly.

"Hello, Gavin?" It was a woman's voice. "This is Pam Burton."

"Hello," I replied. I did not recognize the voice. "What can I do for you?"

There was a pause for a few moments before she spoke again.

"I got your number from the hospital. You have my son's lungs."

### Can we recover your son's organs?

I spoke to Pam for over an hour. She confirmed that she had received my cards and letters and was apologetic about taking so long to respond. Her emotions had been pent up for a long time. Now that she was ready to talk, it flooded out.

Her son, the eldest of two boys, was Noah. He had been enrolled at college in Florida, a bright twenty-two-year-old engineering student. He came home for spring break in early March, and Pam remembered the wonderful time the family spent together. Noah had lost some weight, which he attributed to a bout of flu. Pam remembers how they told him that they loved him and to take care of himself as he drove away. They watched until they could not see his SUV any longer. He had always been in good health, so his family was not unduly concerned.

One evening the following week, Pam received an unexpected phone call. It was the call of every parent's worst nightmare. It was the hospital in Noah's college town. They had dreadful news. Noah was in the emergency room. He had collapsed while taking a shower and was unconscious. Could she come right away?

The next few hours were a blur for Pam and her husband, Eddie. Pam's sister, Reeda, a registered nurse, was visiting from Kentucky and rode with them. They drove frantically for three hours to the hospital in Noah's college town.

On the way, she spoke to one of the doctors at the hospital on her cell phone. The doctor had been reluctant to tell them any specific information. It would be better to talk to them in person when they got to the hospital, he said. Pam couldn't take it. She screamed at the doctor to tell her what was going on. The doctor relented and told her that her son was in a coma and on life-support. The prognosis was not good.

Once at the hospital, the parents were given the devastating news that their son had been pronounced brain-dead. The life-support machine was keeping him breathing, so he looked peaceful and asleep, but there was no possibility that he would recover. The doctors had found a malignant brain tumor that had caused a fatal build-up of intracranial pressure. Pam had to have the concept of brain death explained to her. The doctor explained that it meant the complete loss of brain function. There was not going to be any recovery. Noah was dead.

It was ten o'clock in the evening. Pam and Eddie sat in the hospital waiting room, bewildered, disoriented, and overcome with grief. It had all been so sudden.

A doctor approached. Had they heard of organ donation? he asked gently. Could he explain it to them?

Pam and Eddie listened. Like many people, they had checked the "organ donor" box on their driver's licenses, but they had no direct experience. It was something that only happened to other people. The doctor explained that Noah's organs could be recovered so they could be used to save the lives of seriously ill people. Would they allow them to recover Noah's organs?

Pam and Eddie did not know if Noah was a registered organ donor. He had never talked about it to them. They needed time to think about it.

I'm sorry, the doctor told them, there was not much time. If the organs were going to be recovered, they needed to act quickly. Even now, there was a risk that the organs were deteriorating, and would not be viable much longer for transplant.

Pam knew that Noah was a loving and kind person. She also knew in her heart that her son would want to donate his organs if it meant saving someone's life. Pam and Eddie were consoling each other about the decision they were faced with when they were told that Noah had already made the decision. His driver's license which he had received at sixteen showed the small heart symbol which indicated his consent to be an organ donor.

She and Eddie said yes, okay, what do we need to do?

A flurry of signing consent forms followed. Heart? Liver, pancreas, both kidneys? Both cornea? Both lungs? Intestines? Sign here, here, here, and here, initial here, and here, and date it too, please. It's March 13th. Thank you.

Pam and Eddie were reeling. They were operating on autopilot, unable to adequately process what was going on around them. Noah. Dead?

The skin?

What? She was confused. What about the skin?

Can we recover the skin?

It was too much. The idea of her precious son losing his skin was unfathomable. It was the last straw on the most traumatic and tragic night of her life. No, she said, not the skin. Take the other organs, but not his skin. The unsigned consent form was quietly withdrawn.

The commotion gradually died down. All the forms had been signed. The doctors and hospital staff got on with their duties. Pam and Eddie asked for one final visit with Noah. They said their goodbyes to their beloved son as he lay in the hospital bed with color in his cheeks, eyes closed, and his chest gently rising and falling.

Pam and Eddie were in floods of tears as they left his hospital room. Pam remembers the clank of the ward doors as they closed behind them. It was such a final sound. It was just after midnight on March 14th, 2008. By the strangest of coincidences, it was also Pam's fiftieth birthday.

**Intersection**

When I received my life-saving double-lung transplant on March 14th, a date that is indelibly imprinted in my mind, it was the intersection of my old life with my new life. It is the same date that, while giving so much hope and joy to my family, had delivered such a tragic blow to another family.

I offered to send Pam a copy of my book *Breathe and Let Go: A Lung Transplant Adventure*. While writing the book in 2009, I was acutely aware that it was missing the parallel story of where my lungs came from.

Pam sounded a little surprised, but she gave her home address and I promised to send a copy of the book to her. We finished our conversation and agreed to stay in touch. Neither of us probably knew what "staying in touch" meant under these strange circumstances. I dropped a copy of my book in the mail.

Four days later, I received an email from Pam.

---

**From:** Pam Burton
**Sent:** Wednesday, January 19, 2011 2:12 PM
**To:** Gavin Maitland
**Subject:** Book

Dear Gavin,

I received your book yesterday. I was emotionally overwhelmed when I read the back cover and skimmed through the book yesterday afternoon. Last night I completed the book at 12:30 a.m. You did a wonderful job and it is amazing the trials you and your family went through together.

Hope all is going well with you and I am so happy for you. I am at a better place than I have been in a long time. God really does perform miracles! I just didn't know I would receive one.

Sincerely,
Pam

---

It is often difficult to talk about the benefits of cadaveric organ donation. Who would be an organ donor who did not have to be? A recent press article[28] is an example of how many organs are blocked from being used in transplant - around one hundred every year in the United Kingdom - due to objections from relatives, despite the deceased being a registered organ donor. Laws suggest that although consent may be given by the deceased, the wishes of relatives are respected if they want to block the organ donation.

But in the most tragic of circumstances, allowing the recovery of a loved one's organs can offer a significant degree of solace. The donor family may feel that their loss was not in vain, as it helped someone else to live, albeit a total stranger. In many cases, eight solid organs may be recovered - heart, two kidneys, liver, two lungs, pancreas, and intestine - which may benefit up to eight different recipients; corneas may restore two people's sight, and bones, tendons, skin, heart valves, nerves, and veins which may heal the lives of up to another seventy-five people.[29]Thinking about the direct benefit to others may provide comfort to grieving friends and relatives.

The human stories of donors and recipients are often the most moving. Each organ and each transplant ripples across families and communities. The act of donation can have a far-reaching effect and leave a powerful legacy for all families involved. As well as helping organ recipients, the donation of body parts can help medical research find new therapies and treatments for human diseases. But above all else, organ donation is the ultimate expression of love and generosity.

**Wedding invitation**

Pam and I kept in touch by email. I spoke to her one more time, but she seemed to prefer the distance of periodic emails. We exchanged holiday cards.

She also sent me a head shot photo of Noah. The photo showed a dark haired, smiling, young man. It was an informal

---

28   The Daily Telegraph; 19 October 2017
29   https://www.donatelife.net/statistics/

shot, probably taken without much thought. Who would ever think that a quick photo could be a person's last ever image? I looked at the photo closely. This was the young man who had given his lungs to me. He was dead, but I could feel his still-alive lungs in my chest. I put my hand on my chest to feel my breathing, as I often do when I need to feel grounded. Thank you, Noah, I thought, looking at his face. That photo is the only picture I have of him.

I wanted to meet Pam and her husband, Eddie, to say thank you to them for the priceless gift, although it seemed rather impetuous to get on the next flight to Florida. I felt I needed a reason to visit them. Perhaps they felt the same way.

Two years later, a reason materialized. Pam wrote an email to tell me that her second son, Hunter, my donor's younger brother, was engaged to be married. The wedding was planned for the day of what would have been Noah's twenty-eighth birthday. Would I be able to come?

I accepted without hesitation. It seemed a little extravagant to fly over to Florida to a wedding of people I had never met, but I had a strong impulse to meet them and thank them in person.

Initially, we planned for only Julie and me to travel to Florida. As the date became closer, we found that Riley had an unexpected day off school, so she would be able to come too. The day before we left for the airport, the rain that had been steadily falling in the Boulder area for the past two days became heavier.

Unbeknown to us, the bad weather was developing into the 2013 Colorado Front Range Flood. The fifteen inches of rainfall over the span of a week would cause flooding which would kill eight people and cause billions of dollars in property damage. The weather forecast meant school closures, so Zander was unexpectedly available to come too. We booked a last-minute seat for him on the flight, and all four of us set off to the airport through the torrential rain.

The wedding was held at a golf club in Florida on a Friday evening. The flight had been uneventful, and we rented a car on arrival. We drove to a hotel near the venue. We were dressed and ready by 5:30 p.m. We drove over to the golf club for the 6:00 p.m. start.

I felt nervous to meet the parents of my donor after all this time. It was over five years since my transplant. I had carefully instructed the kids to hang back, as this was a day for the bride and groom, not us.

There was nothing for it but to walk into the club house. I took a deep breath and walked in with Julie, Zander, and Riley.

The first person I met was Pam. I knew immediately who she was. She immediately knew who I was. I walked up to her and put my arms around her. Her eyes welled up with tears. I also met Eddie, Hunter, and Hunter's fiancé. I felt humbled and awe-struck at the same time.

The wedding ceremony was held outdoors in a marquee. The air was humid, and everyone was perspiring. To the relief of all present, the ceremony was short and succinct. Before long, photos were being taken, and guests were retreating to the air-conditioned club house.

A buffet dinner reception has been set up inside, with each of the tables decorated with center pieces and a single framed photograph. The photograph was of Noah. It was an enlargement of the picture I had in my wallet. It was strange to feel that, although he was not there, in a way, he was. He would have been in the thoughts of his parents, his brother, and many relatives, and his lungs were in my chest. It was an awkward feeling. I looked over at Zander and Riley. They were calm and relaxed. Their assuredness gave me confidence.

As the evening got underway, many of the guests approached to introduce themselves. I met uncles, aunts, cousins, and many friends of the bride and groom. There were not many friends of Noah, due to the length of time that had passed since his death. It would have been difficult for his parents to stay in touch with his college friends.

Everyone was friendly and asked the usual pleasantries - when had we arrived, how long were we staying, had we ever been to this part of Florida before? Yes, it's beautiful, I agreed, quite hot and humid, a wonderful venue for a wedding, such a nice ceremony. It was difficult to know if they were genuinely interested, or if there was an element of morbid curiosity behind our presence. Perhaps it was a mix of both. By 11:00 p.m., we had been welcomed as part of the family and even cajoled onto the dance floor.

The following day, Pam invited our family to their home for a brunch with immediate family. It was a good opportunity to talk to her and Eddie without the formality of the wedding. We sat by the swimming pool in the backyard, drinking coffee and talking.

Pam produced a photo album which had many photos and memorabilia of her two boys as they grew up. I could see Noah progress from a baby to a toddler to a child to an adolescent. He was doing all the activities that boys do: birthday parties, fun at the beach, soccer games, music concerts, group family photos, making faces at the camera and being silly. As the pages turned, Pam explained each event and each occasion where Noah had participated. I could tell she found it difficult but, at the same time, she was determined to give me this access to her son.

A thought occurred to me. Did anyone else who was a recipient of his organs contact her? When I was still in hospital, I had been urged to write to thank my donor family. It seemed such an obvious thing to do. Had other recipients done the same?

No, she said quietly, looking right at me. I was the only one. No one else had contacted her.

She looked down again and turned the final page with a photo. There were four or five remaining pages, but they were blank. There were no more photos. It must have been when Noah's life abruptly ended. Pam paused in reflection for a moment, then closed the album and silently took it into the house.

When we left, saying our goodbyes, thank you, so nice to meet you, I could see that Pam was struggling to contain her emotions. It was difficult to know what to say. I was not sure if I should offer to have her put a hand on my chest to feel her son's lungs. In the event, I did not, and she did not ask. It was too delicate. We drove back to our hotel.

About a week later, I received an email from Pam.

**From:** Pam Burton
**Sent:** Friday, September 27, 2013 9:22 AM
**To:** Gavin Maitland
**Subject:** Positive thoughts

Good Morning Gavin,

As I wrote in my previous email, Eddie and I went to a neighborhood committee meeting last night at our neighbor's house. They were at the wedding with several of our other neighbors. Anyway, after business, talk turned to the wedding and then you. Someone mentioned how emotional that must have been for us, and I said yes, but it was a good emotional feeling.

What I told them is something I want to share with you, so you will know the effect your family's attendance had on me personally. Bedtime can be very hard. All is quiet and if I don't fall immediately to sleep, my mind goes to Noah and the tragic time at the emergency room and my first glimpse of Noah dead but on life support to keep his organs alive (which made it look like he was still breathing and alive).

All the images of that night, the long 3+ hour drive, the phone calls from the hospital to see how close we were, and the ones to immediate family (especially his brother) and the long drive back home in the wee hours are still so vivid. Thank God, my sister was with us for her strong support. She was here to celebrate a surprise 50th birthday party (my first) on the 14th with our neighbors. Eddie had gotten me my gold thumb ring for my birthday, so I dearly love this ring for what it now represents to me.

The last few nights of this week when all the images start coming, when I usually cry, my thoughts have gone forward to you. Now it seems when I start thinking of all the events of the tragedy, I turn to the blessing of you and your life. I now end up with happy thoughts to fall asleep and I just want you to know how special you are to me. To finally get to meet you, Julie, Zander, and Riley have had the most positive affect on me emotionally and I thank you.

Love,
Pam

John Wooden, the legendary basketball player and coach once said, "You can't live a perfect day without doing something for someone who will never be able to repay you."

I received something from the Burton family – a gift I will never be able to repay.

**Ten years on**

Approaching the tenth anniversary of Noah's passing and my lung transplant, I arranged to speak to Pam by telephone in January 2018.

In some ways, a decade seemed like a long time. In other ways, it seemed very short. Vivid events often retain a rawness that is not dulled by the passing of time. Pam is also living with a double-tragedy as her husband of thirty-six years, and Noah and Hunter's father, Eddie, died in May 2017, after a protracted battle with lung cancer.

Pam described Noah's character and personality. "Noah was very smart," she began. "I've had lots of people come up to me over the years to talk about how exceptional he was.

He was very family-oriented. When Noah was two, he would much rather be in a room of adults than with his peers. He was very advanced for his years. He had a dry humor. He and his Dad were like two peas in a pod. He was friendly, he cared for people, but he didn't have to be around a lot of people. He was comfortable with himself. Put him in front of the computer, he would be happy for hours."

With the perspective of ten years, I asked her how she felt about the decision she and Eddie made to donate Noah's organs. I wondered what Noah would have thought about that decision.

"I am so proud of Noah," she said. "When he got his driver's license, he made the designation to be an organ donor. Eddie and I didn't even have to make the decision, although we didn't realize it. We made the decision to donate his organs, then found out that it was out of our hands, as he had already done that. I'm so proud that was done. Noah would have been thrilled to know that someone like you got his lungs."

I asked if there is anything she would have done differently.

"If we could have done anything differently, it was the tissue donation," she went on. "When they asked about it, I said no because, of course, that is the time when he was still lying there, and I just couldn't think of them taking his skin off. Now I have read and seen different things on television about how wonderful that is for people. In hindsight, if I had to do it again, I would also donate the skin and tissue."

I asked if she could describe her decision to reach out to me, a recipient of one of Noah's organs. It cannot have been easy.

"I had received the letters from you and your family – the drawing from your children. It really touched me," she said. "It helped me realize that even if we had lost Noah, your kids got to keep their father. It meant a lot. I reached out because I needed to talk to you. It also helped me feel connected with Noah. Outside of memories, it was pretty much the last thing we had of him. And you have it. It was a way to be close to Noah without being able to be."

Once we were in contact, I asked her to describe how it affected her.

131

"Any effect was positive," she said. "It was so great to meet you and to be able to put faces to names. When I hugged you, I felt I was hugging Noah. I felt that Noah was there."

I asked her to comment on her faith. Was there ever a time when she questioned her faith?

"I never questioned my faith," she said firmly. "I have always believed in God the Father, Jesus the Son, and the Holy Spirit in us. I have always believed in the Trinity. That never wavered, although I was not fully committed at that time. Of course, I kept asking why. I still ask why. I don't understand. I know that God has a plan. When I get up there, He is going to have to explain it to me."

She paused for a moment before continuing. "Since then, my faith has grown more so. Over the past three or four years, for Eddie and me, it only became stronger. We both knew that we will see Noah again. After Eddie got sick again, he said he wasn't afraid to die. The bad part was leaving Hunter and me, but he knew he was going to be with his Lord and Noah. He was okay with it, the sicker he got. I know right now that he and Noah are up there. Probably golfing." She laughed gently.

"When Noah died, I didn't feel my faith was as deep," she went on. "I relied on alcohol to ease my pain. I'm proud to say I haven't had a drink since December 2013. With Eddie's illness, which went on for a year-and-a-half, I have leaned on my faith and church family. It has helped tremendously. I feel so much stronger. They say the worst thing that can happen to parents is to lose a child. I agree with that but, when we lost Noah, I still had Eddie. We comforted each other."

I asked if there is any advice she would offer to a family who is faced with a similar decision regarding organ donation.

"There is no downside to organ donation," she said. "There is nothing negative about it. I have heard people talking about disfiguring the body and all that. Well, the thing is, it is just a body. The person is not there anymore. The fulfilment it gives you after the fact is like a miracle. To have been a part of that miracle, to be able to see that happen, is amazing. I can't imagine anybody not wanting to help another human, and it lets your family member live on."

Noah Burton.
September 13th, 1985 – March 13th, 2008

# CHAPTER TEN: NEW YORK HARBOR SWIM

*"Cement shoes. A largely fictional method of execution and/ or body disposal, usually associated with criminals such as the Mafia. It involves weighting down the victim, who may be dead or alive, with concrete and throwing them into the water in the hope the body will never be found. In the US, the term has become tongue-in-cheek for a threat of death by criminals. Only one real-life case is confirmed."*

- Wikipedia

**Eight years post-transplant:**
**braving hazards to swim across New York harbor**

"If you see a dead body in the water, make sure you tell one of the kayakers!" The wetsuited man next to us grinned to his friends.

Riley and I looked at each other and laughed. The setting was the 2016 Lady Liberty swim, a one-point-six-mile swim crossing of Upper New York Harbor from the base of the Statue of Liberty to the New Jersey State Park on July 16th, 2016.

The Mafia-type reference to cement shoes was dark humor indeed. The man was one of a hundred or so athletes who had congregated at 6:30 a.m. on this warm Saturday morning at the marina in Liberty State Park. Everyone was excited to be part of a memorable open-water swim.

"We have one hundred and ten swimmers this morning," boomed the lead-organizer, a huge man with a bright red sweatshirt. "Once all the athletes are aboard the ferry, it will head out into the bay and over to the statue."

The swim would start at Liberty Island, the epicenter of where the Hudson River meets the East River at the southern tip of Manhattan Island. It was undoubtedly one of the few times that anyone would voluntarily jump from a perfectly good ship into the New York waterways. The pre-swim briefing continued, the organizer's voice thundering out over the sea of eager yellow swim caps.

"Once we get out on the water, listen for instructions. On my command, make your way to the back of the ferry and get ready to jump. It's a water start. Once you're in the water, swim to the green kayaks that mark the start and hang tight. When everyone is in position, we'll start the swim!"

About a quarter of the swimmers were not wearing wetsuits. The water temperature was officially declared as being seventy-one degrees[30], so the cold was not prohibitive. Today, Riley was wearing her wetsuit. I was not.

I have lived in the United States for fifteen years and am familiar with storied national landmarks such as The Washington Monument, Mount Rushmore, or The Golden Gate Bridge. But I am still fascinated by the most famous of them all, the Statue of Liberty.

Whether it is how it was built in France, then gifted to the United States in 1886, or how it represented hope for nineteenth century immigrants, or the special emotional place it occupies as a symbol of all-things American, I don't know. The roughest of sketches of the statue immediately says America - just as an image of the Eiffel Tower says France or the Taj Mahal says India - like no other symbol.

Laying my eyes on the statue was my top priority the first time I visited New York City as a teenager. I clearly remember standing in Battery Park, looking out across the harbor at the distant silhouette, mesmerized by its three-hundred-foot presence across the clear blue water.

Or perhaps the water was not as clear as I remembered. In contrast to our previous year's swim across San Francisco Bay, where the most common question was about the presence of sharks, the most common question about a New York swim was about pollution. Typically, "You're swimming in the New York harbor? Eeww!"

I had registered for this event the year before as a preparatory open-water swim prior to the bridge-to-bridge swim. Riley had been otherwise committed, so I was determined to swim without

---

30  21°C

her – much to her chagrin. As I prepared to board the flight to LaGuardia Airport the day before, I received an email from the organizers to say that the event had been canceled because of bad weather.

Bad weather? It hardly seemed possible. Rain showers had been forecast for New York on Friday, but that would be an unlikely reason for a cancelation, especially as the forecast for the day of the swim was clear skies. It was only later that the real reason for the cancellation was disclosed. It was both water and weather-related.

With over eight million residents squeezed into three hundred square miles, New York City is easily the most densely populated major city in the United States. The city's water supply system is one of the world's most extensive. Unsurprisingly, population growth has put a lot of stress on the city's infrastructure. When rainfall enters the storm drains, it usually flows directly to sewage treatment plants, but the combined flows from sewers and storm drains often exceed the treatment plants' capacity. This in turn can cause the overflow of untreated waste into the surrounding rivers, including the Hudson.

And that's not all. According to New York State's Department of Environmental Conservation, pollution runoff is an even bigger problem. Rain sweeps dog waste and other trash into the nearest storm drain, which then flows into the rivers. This waste moves through the food chain until it settles in the river fish. The bad news is that humans can be significantly exposed to these pollutants by regularly eating Hudson River fish. The good news, at least for swimmers, is that swallowing a few mouthfuls of water is not generally hazardous in itself[31].

The New York Department of Health's website offers advice. Apart for the obvious aquatic hazards, such as drowning or being on the wrong end of a jet ski - not to minimize these hazards, but at least they can be somewhat mitigated - the website advises swimmers to consider keeping face and head out of the water

31  "How is the Hudson Doing?" http://www.dec.ny.gov/lands/77105. html (accessed 11/28/2017)

completely to minimize exposure to "bacteria, parasites, blue-green algae, and other microorganisms." It also advises washing hands after swimming and to shower to "wash off river water and dirt."

While the hazards were noted and accepted, I still wanted to know it was safe enough to swim. In response to the question "Can I Swim in the Hudson?", New York State's official word is "Generally, yes". That was good enough for me.

To me, the answer to the existential question about whether to swim or not to swim was unequivocal: swim. Just don't swallow too much water.

## No more swimming

In the weeks after my transplant, I remember thinking that I would like to get back to swimming. Like many former college athletes, I found that if I was not training and competing, then I did not see the point in recreational swimming. Jogging took less time, needed less gear, and kept me in good shape. All I needed was my running shoes, and I could squeeze in a run wherever I was. By the time I was in the post-transplant phase in 2008, I had not swum regularly for nearly twenty years.

At one of the weekly post-transplant consultations at Duke, one of the team of pulmonologists underlined the importance of maintaining a regular post-transplant exercise regimen. "You know, brisk walking, stretching, light weights, that kind of thing," he said. "At least every other day."

"What about swimming?" I asked.

He paused for a moment.

"Well, there's nowhere more filled with bacteria than a swimming pool," he said with a disparaging smile. "You're immunocompromised. Avoid it completely."

"No swimming at all?"

"Yes, avoid it completely. There are plenty of other ways you can stay fit."

I was more than a little disappointed. I hated to idea of being prohibited from getting back in the water. At the following week's consultation, I sat before a different pulmonologist. I thought I would try again.

"What about swimming?" I asked hopefully.

"Hmm, swimming," he looked thoughtful. "I competed in a triathlon last year. Great work out."

Ah-ha. He was an athlete. It was far more likely he would understand.

"But pools have lots of germs," he went on. "Where were you thinking of swimming?"

"In the sea?" I offered quickly, thinking of somewhere that was not an indoor swimming pool. Besides, North Carolina is the home to some of the most fabulous beaches on the Atlantic coast, so residents are generally familiar with sea-swimming.

"Yes, that should be fine," he said.

"And a pool?" I asked. I was probably pushing my luck.

"It's a bit of a balance," he said. "Your immune system is compromised, so of course there is risk from bacteria in swimming pools. But there are also undoubted cardiovascular benefits from exercising. And swimming is a great way to use your new lungs. You need to weigh the risks and strike the right balance."

I was nodding expectantly. I'm sure he knew what I wanted him to say.

He seemed to concede. "Yes, I guess, okay, a pool should be fine. Try not to swallow any water. But lake swimming is out. Far too much bacteria."

"Great," I said. "Thanks!" I had a green light.

## Manhattan skyline

Once in position next to the towering green statue, we discarded our outer garments and filed to the ferry's stern. On command, and still talking, swimmers jumped in, one after the other, like a colony of penguins leaping off an ice flow.

The water felt wonderfully soft and warm on my skin. Riley and I treaded water together as our fellow athletes assembled around us, the air filled with chatter and anticipation. As the horn went off, I wished her luck. From previous swims, we knew we could not keep track of one another during the swim, so agreed to meet at the finish.

I wiped the fog from my goggles, took a deep breath, and eased into freestyle. Ahead, the classic Manhattan skyline was breathtaking. Aim for the landmark of the Goldman Sachs Tower, they had told us. The giant and unmistakable forty-four-story silhouette - exactly twice the height of the Statue of Liberty - made easy sighting in the distance.

The bright sun pierced my eyes as I turned my head to the right to breath. One of the motorized support boats sped by, a little too close for comfort. I could smell the diesel fumes across the water. I switched to my left side to breathe for the next and following inhalations as I rode out the swell caused by the vessel.

A continuous swim allowed me to focus on my stroke. That may sound strange, as many people believe that swimming is one-dimensional, like upright walking, except in the water. Not so. The more I swim, the more I find that swimming provides an unlimited opportunity for challenge and improvement.

Several years before, I took a six-week instructor-led course on the swimming technique known as "Total Immersion." This technique was developed by Terry Laughlin. Its focus is to teach swimmers to use balance and a streamlined shape to use less energy and gain more propulsion, and so swim faster and with less fatigue over longer distances.

The technique is appealing to many athletes, not least because its movement and concentration are like meditative activities, such as yoga or martial arts. These arts are practiced, as opposed to just done. Total Immersion teaches swimming as an art of continuous improvement and, to use one of Terry Laughlin's phrases, "mindful practice."

I enjoy using the technique to reduce drag - the swimmer's arch-enemy - by focusing on keeping my body as streamlined as possible. As Terry Laughlin would say, "It's not the size of the engine that's important, it's the shape of the vessel."

For me, that means keeping my head, shoulders, hips and legs in line and level with the water's surface and leaning forward as I swim. Because our legs are usually heavier than our head and upper body, I focus on keeping my weight forward - literally balancing myself on my lungs - to keep my legs higher, my body aligned, and streamlined.

I probably have a greater appreciation of the work and position of my lungs than most people, so I find the visualization of leaning forward in the water to be positive and energizing. As such, my mind is so focused on my position in the water that time passes quickly.

I could see that Manhattan was much closer. I had lost Riley long ago among the specks of swimmers and support kayaks. The early morning swell of the harbor had subsided, and the water felt easy to swim through. I felt pleased that my strokes were strong and consistent, and that my breathing was calm and rhythmic. Occasionally, I could feel a gentle touch on my outstretched hands, only to discover it was the mild and harmless sting of a passing jellyfish. The swim was going to be over far too quickly.

Simon Griffiths, the founder and owner of the London-based publication, *Outdoor Swimmer*, offered to publish a piece about our New York harbor swim. He thought it would be interesting to his adventurous readers, although he was a little skeptical about the length of the swim.

"It's such a short swim," he said. "My readers will wonder why we're featuring it. Let's emphasize the lung transplant angle."

I am always open to talking about my lung transplant. I appreciate how much inspiration I have gained from other lung transplant recipients during my recovery, and I have always felt it my duty to offer inspiration and encouragement to anyone in a tough spot. It was ironic that Simon was down-playing the length of the swim, considering that over half of Americans cannot swim for twenty-five meters. However, on reflection, considering the magazine's diehard readership, perhaps this swim did seem a bit paltry.

## Ellis Island

Ellis Island was coming into view on my left. I could barely see my outstretched hand due to the cloudiness of the water as

I pushed forward with each stroke. I was also aware that there were no other swimmers around me. I could see three or four yellow caps in the distance in front and the same number even further behind. I could not see any kayaker nearby either.

It doesn't bother me not to have any up-close support. You can swim a long way in the pool and not get into any difficulty, so logically, the open water should not be any different. No need to dwell on what could be beneath me.

It seemed incredible: I was swimming past Ellis Island! The gateway for over seventeen million immigrants into the United States for over sixty years from 1892 to 1954 glowed in the sunlight. To think: around forty percent of all current American citizens can trace at least one ancestor's arrival on Ellis Island.

As I turned my head each stroke to inhale, I could see every detail of the building's intricate reddish brickwork and its two ornate towers. The main building was designed in the style of the French Renaissance and shone in the sunlight. I wanted to freeze the image in my mind's eye as I swam past the celebrated island that morning.

The swim was almost over. I turned ninety degrees left into the narrow harbor strip that led to the last five hundred yards to the finish line. The water in this protected inlet was perfectly calm but felt much grimier than the open water. I focused on keeping my mouth firmly closed as I rolled my head to avoid taking in any of the silty water. So far, so good, but there was no point in inhaling more toxins than I already had at this late stage.

I arrived at the finish sign and reached out for the ladder. I pulled myself up and out of the water. *Terra firma*. Wonderful.

I had covered the distance in just over fifty-eight minutes, and still felt strong. Swimming is such a great sport, as it brings out such happiness and optimism in everyone. My fellow competitors were milling around, drying off, laughing and joking. Soon, there would be a short impromptu medal ceremony, honoring the first three finishers in each age category, male and female (although no distinction between wetsuited and non-wetsuited competitors). It would be a satisfying end to the swim event.

Riley had unsurprisingly finished well ahead of me and placed second in her age-group, 20th overall. I placed fourth in my age-group, 53rd overall, meaning that I finished in the top half - only just - of a field of 110 swimmers. Again, not being last was an achievement in itself.

I was reunited with Julie and Riley, clutching towels and beaming.

"See any dead bodies?" Riley was deadpan.

"No, you?"

She smiled. "Dad!"

New York Harbor. Riley, Gavin & Julie.
July 2016

New York Harbor. Gavin & Riley.
July 2016

# CHAPTER ELEVEN: GIVING BACK

*"The entire institution of gift giving make no sense. Let's say that I go out, and I spend 50 dollars on you, it's a laborious activity, because I have to imagine what you need, where as you know what you need. Now I could simplify things, just give you the 50 dollars directly, and you could give me 50 dollars on my birthday, and so on, until one of us dies, leaving the other one old and 50 dollars richer. And I ask, is it worth it?"*

- Dr Sheldon Cooper, *The Big Bang Theory* on CBS

## Extraordinary people and organizations giving back

No one can tell you how to give back. You know it is important and you need to figure out what you can do. A year after my life-saving transplant I started writing about my experience. It turned out that writing was cathartic as it allowed me to express the emotion of the transplant roller coaster ride. The writing turned into a book. So far, so good, but I did not really know where to go from there.

Woody Allen once quipped that "showing up is eighty percent of life." Simply by doing something and by taking some action, you can make a meaningful contribution. I decided to show up.

I signed up for a weekend class with the intriguing title "How to Speak for Fun & Profit." The quirky class, along with confidence-building tips and strategies, came with a directory of email addresses of local clubs, societies, senior centers, and high schools, which we were told were eagerly looking for speakers. A flurry of emails later, I lined up a string of breakfast and lunchtime speaking appointments.

I spoke at about fifty events over the following twelve months – averaging about one per week – where I would join the regular meeting of these various clubs, societies, associations, senior centers, and high school classes in Colorado as a guest speaker. In short, I spoke to any audience that would have me.

I honed a pithy twenty-minute talk, so I could belt out an animated summary of my transplant experience at a moment's notice. The talk covered what I had gone through, what I had learned, as well as answering rudimentary questions. I always emphasized that I was not talking from any medical basis, but as a layman.

Most people were probably hazily aware of the concept of organ transplant, with kidney transplant being of course the most well-known. Famous names who have undergone an organ transplant – liver transplants for Mickey Mantel in 1995, George Best in 2002, and Steve Jobs in 2009, a heart transplant for Dick Cheney in 2012, and a directed kidney transplant for Selena Gomez in 2017 - undoubtedly helped to publicize the cause, but a sizable minority of any audience were unaware of the intricacies of organ transplant.

By speaking to increase awareness, I believed I could potentially influence more people to register as organ donors. If nothing else, I prompted people into thinking about it. A common question I was asked, especially by older audiences, was "should I specify in my will my desire to donate my organs upon death?" The answer to this question is, of course, yes, and I would explain.

Let's say you are the victim of a serious car accident. You are still alive when you are taken to the Emergency Room late at night, but the doctors must break the dreadful news to your anxious family that you have not survived. At that point, who is going to have the presence of mind to go back home, open your safe, pull out your will, find the section that deals with your final wishes, and relay that information back to the hospital? Answer: no one!"

What should you do?

Tell someone! Tell your wife, your husband, your boyfriend, your girlfriend, or your children that, in the awful event of an untimely death, you give permission for your organs to be donated. Tell someone!

I often related the story of my donor, and how his parents did not know their dead son's wishes for certain. When they found his driver's license, they felt overwhelmed with relief that *he* had already decided to donate his organs, so they did not have to make the decision. A burden was lifted from their shoulders.

Reactions varied from curiosity to astonishment to humor ("I had no idea they could do lung transplants" to "where do they get the lungs?" to "my wife says I should get a brain transplant, haw haw"). I believe that I may have contributed to increasing awareness of organ transplant, while at the same time livening up a hum-drum lunchtime meeting. Everyone generally listened politely to my talks, asked some questions, and seemed interested. The most receptive audiences were high school students.

I was invited to several high schools and spoke to students in junior and senior grades (sixteen to eighteen-year-olds). Students are a great audience, as they make no attempt to mask what they are thinking. Their facial expressions and body language tell you if they are bored. Equally, if they are interested, they listen with intensity and ask perceptive questions. Guidance from a committed teacher makes a huge impact.

## Leslie Durant

Everyone should have had a teacher like Mrs. Durant. I met Leslie Durant when I contacted several high schools in the Denver-metro area to offer to speak to students about organ transplant. She is the Science Department Leader at Arvada High School in Colorado and gushes with enthusiasm and fascination for her subject.

I first spoke to her science class in 2010 about my lung transplant experience and have spoken to one of her classes almost every year since. Students are intrigued by the medicine and science of an organ transplant, but also by the human aspect of the donor - often a young person like them - and the logistics of organ recovery.

"Many of my students aren't exposed to organ transplant unless one of their friends or relatives has received a donated organ," she said. "Sometimes the only time they are asked about it is when they apply for a driver's license. I think knowledge is power – and after talking about it to my students, they can feel powerful over their own body and, at the same time, make an informed decision."

The students derive a benefit from seeing and hearing an organ transplant recipient guest speaker in person. "It becomes real to students to hear an organ transplant recipient tell his or her story and make a connection through words," she said. "Seeing someone right in front of them who benefits from organ donation every day pulls them in and engages them."

## Winter Vinecki

When Zander and Riley were growing up, they competed in a series of kids' triathlons in Colorado. At one of these events, they met a young athlete, Winter Vinecki, who was a regular feature on the medalists' podium. As well as being a world-class athlete, she had a compelling story.

When she was nine years old, her father was diagnosed with an aggressive form of prostate cancer and died within months. The absence of a visible prostate cancer awareness movement gave the young athlete an idea. Winter, her brothers and her mother, Dawn, committed to a non-profit organization, Team Winter,[32] which raises funds for prostate cancer awareness and research.

In an online post, Winter wrote, "I love inspiring youth across America to live an active, positive, healthy lifestyle, and to race not only for themselves but for a cause."

While athletes and their families were milling around at the end of a triathlon, Winter would invariably take to the stage with a microphone and deliver a brief but hard-hitting talk on her motivation and cause. "Ladies!" she would yell out. "Prostate cancer is a killer. Look after your man!" As she wrapped up her talk, she would lock eye-contact with the audience and intensely conclude, "Ask yourself, who do you race for?"

Winter's example was one of action. It's not enough to think about action, you must do something. She must have struck a

---

32  More information at www.teamwinter.org

chord. The 2015 Bridge-to-bridge swim was my family's first real attempt to fundraise for organ transplant causes.

## Steve Farber

If you want an example of giving back through taking action, talk to Steve Farber. He is a founding partner of a prominent law firm, managing offices in eleven cities across the United States, as well as being involved in many political, charitable, and community causes. In 2004, he received a life-saving kidney transplant from his eldest son. The year after his transplant, he founded the Denver-based American Transplant Foundation.[33]

I had the opportunity to talk with Steve Farber in January 2018 and asked him why he started the American Transplant Foundation.

"It was focused on one of my many trips to the hospital," he said. "I knew that if I survived there was something I owed to people who were supportive. I asked, what could I do?"

"The most obvious donors were my kids, although there were so many other issues with the family. Are you subjecting your family to future issues by encouraging someone to be a donor? I am not sure, even today. My oldest son became a donor and thankfully he's healthy." He paused to touch the desk with his knuckles. "I knock on wood every day," he said.

Has the American Transplant Foundation achieved what he wanted it to achieve? "We're still trying to encourage people to become donors at levels far greater than we've succeeded," he said. "However, the success we have had is significant. Did we save a lot of lives? Yes. Did we do the right thing? I answer that, yes."

At the outset of 2018, the national transplant waiting list stands at approximately 116,000 individuals in the United States[34], approximately ninety-five percent of whom could benefit from a living donation of a kidney or part of a liver. Another name is added to the national list every ten minutes and, on average,

33  More information at www.americantransplantfoundation.org
34  Source: www.americantransplantfoundation.org/about-transplant/facts-and-myths

twenty people die every day waiting for an organ transplant. The pace of change is undeniably frustrating.

"There is still more to do," he acknowledged.

## Anastasia Henry

Anastasia Henry, the executive director of the American Transplant Foundation, is in her late thirties with a friendly smile that masks a steely determination. She speaks fluently and passionately with a slight accent from her native Russia. Asked to describe the objectives of the American Transplant Foundation, she responded that its mission was to save lives of men, women and kids on the transplant waiting list.

"We believe that the most efficient way to save lives is through a three-tiered approach of education, emotional support, and financial support. We are a community-based organization, and we provide real help to real families. We work with family members, loved ones, friends, as well as living donors and potential living donors," she said.

It is obvious that her role is much more than a job. She is animated and heartfelt. "First of all, we provide a mentorship service. We match anyone who is on the transplant wait list, or about to go on the list, or who is thinking about donating an organ. It's a national program and we have over a hundred trained mentors. Last year, we had mentor-mentee matches in forty-one states. The program was started in 2014 and we already had fifty surgeries through this program."

Where else does American Transplant Foundation offer help?

"In addition to mentorship, we provide educational resources and financial grants, which is unique, as we support transplant patients with anti-rejection medication," she said. "We all understand how critical it is to give patients consistent access to anti-rejection medication.

"We also know how incredibly expensive these drugs can be, and if you don't take them for a week, you might lose your organ. We created a program that helps to bridge the gap and provide financial assistance, so patients can afford health insurance."

"Unfortunately, there are often limited resources available. Often other organizations run out of funds by June or July, and then their patients come to us. It's a big responsibility.

"At the same time, we are a small organization and depend on individual donors, so it's important that people who are passionate about it can join our monthly giving program. They can cycle, they can run, and they can truly be ambassadors for the thousands of transplant patients who are on the list. The biggest fear that we have is that we run out of funds and we won't be able to be there for these families," she said.

"Awareness is amazing and much needed, but we also believe that without support for patients and their families, it's not a complete system. If we raise awareness, we also need to raise resources."

To put her comments into context, she was referring to the significant proportion of the national organ transplant waiting list who could benefit from a kidney or liver transplant. Anastasia corrected my terminology. When a kidney or part of a liver is donated by a living donor to a stranger, the appropriate term is an "altruistic" or "non-directed" donation. A donor may or may not ever meet the recipient. On the other hand, a "directed" donation goes to a known person, such as a relative, a friend, someone a donor may have met on social media, or even seen on television.

The work of the American Transplant Foundation is important to Anastasia personally. "About a month before I joined, I lost my mom to cancer," she said. "It was a long battle. All I wanted to do was to be the doctor who came up with a solution for my mom."

"I came across Steve Farber's book, *On The List,* when I was going to Russia to see my mom for the last time. I was so fascinated by transplantation and how it is truly a second chance at life."

"And we already have a solution," she said. "But the road to this solution is so challenging. If people like Steve Farber were having challenges, what about someone like my mom? It was like a lightbulb. Wow, we can make a difference! It wasn't about finding a cure "one day." The cure is already here!"

In terms of giving back, Anastasia is passionate about providing what she calls "real help." "

"Of course, we encourage people to learn about the miracle of transplant, registering as on organ donor and learning about living donation. But sometimes providing real help through financial support can be as valuable as donating an organ. "Financial support can fund up to twenty people who are able to step-up and become living donors," she said.

From my own transplant experience, the turnaround from pre- to post-transplant was the closest thing I have ever come to magic. In a matter of months, I went from being too ill to walk, or even brush my teeth, to being back to a healthy and productive member of society. If an organ transplant is considered "magic" or a miracle, it is unfortunately often the result of a tragedy.

"But living donation can be a miracle without a tragedy," said Anastasia.

### Jeff Goldstein

The Lung Transplant Foundation (LTF)[35], is a non-profit organization founded in 2009 by lung transplant recipients. The powerhouse behind the organization is its president and founding member, Jeffrey R. Goldstein, himself a lung transplant recipient.

The LTFs mission is to advocate and raise funds for lung transplant research, as well as providing education and emotional support for transplant recipients and their caregivers through its mentorship program. To get some inside information, I caught up with Jeff by phone at the start of February 2018.

Jeff described his motivation behind setting up the foundation and expanded on its role in helping lung transplant recipients.

"I was forty-three when I was transplanted in 2003," he said. "I started getting calls from spouses of friends and transplant coordinators. I remember specifically a young man who was having troubles pre-transplant whom the doctors asked me to

---

35   More information at www.lungtransplantfoundation.org

help mentor through the program. I helped him through it and he got his life together. Then I got a call from my transplant coordinator to tell me that they were taking him off life-support. That kind of thing happens far too frequently."

"I knew what I was getting into when I went for a transplant," he went on. "I knew that the survival statistics were the poorest of all solid organ transplants and that getting past one year was a real landmark. I was hoping I would make three, maybe five years. I started thinking "why does this happen to us?"

"The most obvious answer is that the respiratory tract starts at your nose and everything goes right into your lungs. Of all the solid organs that are transplanted, lungs are the only ones that are exposed to the outside environment. That makes us highly susceptible to infection, and we are immunocompromised."

"Not only do we have rejection and infection issues, but we also have this insidious disease called bronchiolitis obliterans syndrome (BOS). If you get it, it's a real problem. Every day I wake up grateful, and then fearful, that today could be the day it starts.

"Doctors respond by throwing everything they can at it, as quickly as they can. If it doesn't work, you're in a heap of trouble. You either die or, if you're fortunate, you may be re-transplanted."

Investigating the issue, Jeff looked around to see if there was any organization or pharmaceutical company looking to develop therapies to treat BOS. He related how all the organizations he found were raising money for pre-transplant diseases, such as cystic fibrosis, idiopathic pulmonary fibrosis, and Alpha-1. He found that there was little conversation about these diseases being end-stage lung disease, and that patients were ultimately going to need a lung transplant.

"I guess it must be me," he said. "I had to do something. It was as much for me as for the rest of my friends, and the community."

"It was a lot smaller back then. In 2003, we were eight or nine hundred lung transplants in the entire country – a small community with poor outcomes. I understood the economics from the pharmaceutical side. It's a small patient population and it costs millions of dollars to develop therapies. I thought we could raise money, fund research and develop drugs for our community."

"All this spurred me. Perhaps naively, I thought we could fund research for post-transplant complications, rejection, BOS, and actually develop a pharmaceutical therapy. That's why I formed the foundation."

Jeff related how the foundation was built primarily by lung transplant patients and their caregivers. The problem with that structure was that lung transplant patients pass away from complications such as rejection and BOS. In the first five years, Jeff remembers how he lost three board members.

"Cut ahead to where we are now," he said. "We recognize that our population is usually financially challenged, and resources are drained. It's a challenge financially, because of the cost of drugs, health insurance and home-care," he said.

"It's difficult for us to raise funds, so we try to unite our patient population and use our leverage to build a series of connections to leverage those opportunities."

The book *The Tipping Point*[36] describes how people and organizations make connections, which is how Jeff believes he can best serve the community. As described by author Malcolm Gladwell, *connectors* know large numbers of people and who introduce people who live or work in different circles. They are the social equivalent of a computer network hub.

Jeff provided some specific examples. "I spoke to a company in the FDA regulatory process that is developing a pharmaceutical agent for treating BOS in end-of-life uses," he said. "We introduced them to three doctors in large transplant centers who were excited about the opportunity. They intend to develop a process to test this pharmacological agent for BOS, which is part of the process to get FDA approval."

"I have spent the last six years building the reputation of the LTF to make people aware that this organization is about

---

36 "The Tipping Point: How Little Things Can Make a Big Difference" by Malcolm Gladwell (Little, Brown 2000)

encouraging cures and developing therapies. Part of our mission statement is to help develop therapies which make the lives of post-transplant patients easier and better."

There are a number of ways in which someone could support the foundation's efforts. "I can always ask for money," he said. "Money allows us to continue to build our organization, which is important, since we are a small population. Financial support allows us to go to events and build programs for our community."

Financial support helps the foundation's executive team and board of directors reach out to organizations that can focus on developing therapies, like the American Thoracic Society (ATS), the American Society of Transplantation (AST), and The International Society for Heart & Lung Transplantation (ISHLT). These are the professional medical organizations in this arena that are looking to share research and develop therapies.

"We go to these events and practice one of my favorite terms "advocate and agitate." When I need to cajole people into doing things, I'm not afraid of telling them," he said.

Jeff mentioned that several organizations are currently advancing products through the research and regulatory process, including medical devices, such as tools for bronchoscopy. For example, he was introduced to a company at the ATS meeting which is developing a diagnostic technique to predict which patients will get BOS. The results from small study populations are encouraging. Early diagnosis means early treatment, which means better outcomes. Jeff believes that building these types of connections helps him to move research forward.

"Our community is diverse," he pointed out. "We are all over the country. To build a bigger and broader community, we have embarked on a chapter development program. This is the method by which most of the organizations in the pre-transplant community work with. I would rather have somebody call me and say they want to start a chapter than write a check. Involvement is critical. There are not enough of us to do this alone."

I asked Jeff his views on his own survival, as he is fourteen-and-a-half years post-transplant. "If you ask fifty of us, you will get fifty different answers," he laughed. "For me, it's what I do.

It keeps me focused and drives me. It gives me energy. It's what I wake up for in the morning."

"Secondly, as busy as I am, I maintain a post-rehabilitation regimen – yoga, light weight-lifting, and walking. I live in a three-story house and take the stairs all the time. I think that activity is critical," he said.

He summarized his philosophy by quoting a line from his all-time favorite movie, *The Shawshank Redemption*, which is "Get busy living or get busy dying."[37]

"What a great line!" he said.

## Chris Klug

"Any athletic events coming up?" a fellow-guest asked recently at a dinner. "Swimming any oceans, scaling any mountains?" Did I detect a hint of sarcasm? Some sedentary friends and acquaintances couldn't get their heads around some of my antics.

Ignoring the tone, I pretended to think for a moment. "Well, actually…"

That weekend I was planning to compete in a walk/run up Aspen Mountain on Saturday evening. When I told him, I added, "It's an event to raise awareness for organ donation. A few hundred competitors start at the base of Aspen mountain and race to the summit."

"But it's December," he said, blankly.

"Yes, I know. It's a race in the dark."

"Blind-folded too? Incredulity and skepticism at the same time.

"No," I replied. "Just in the dark."

The event I was anticipating was the *Summit for Life*, an annual fundraiser organized and hosted by Chris Klug and his eponymous foundation[38]. Chris is a four-time World Cup winner, six-time US National Champion, a US Open winner, and a three-time snowboarding Olympian.

---

37  Line delivered by both Andy Dufresne, played by Tim Robbins, and by "Red" Redding, played by Morgan Freeman, in *The Shawshank Redemption* (directed by Frank Darabont, 1994).

38  www.chrisklugfoundation.org

By winning a bronze medal at the 2002 Winter Olympics in Salt Lake City he has the unusual distinction of being the world's only organ transplant recipient - he received a liver in 2000 - to have won an Olympic medal. In person, he is a gregarious, six feet four, larger-than-life character. I have never seen him without a broad smile on his face.

Among other things, his prolific foundation reaches teenagers through *Donor Dudes*, a national grassroots high school and college outreach program to help educate and raise awareness about the importance of organ donation.

Lauren Pierce is the executive director of the foundation and shares Chris' passion. "CKF just celebrated fifteen years," she said.

"The foundation has registered thousands of people and educated even more. Using our online curriculum that is in schools from coast to coast, we can provide young adults with facts about organ donation, so they can make an informed decision."

The foundation has reached over two million people in their effort to "eliminate the wait," according to Lauren. It strives to lead the way in increasing registration, educating as many people as possible, and helping to inspire not only those going through the transplant process, but anyone trying to overcome a challenge.

Chris described his motivation behind the creation of the foundation. "I was in a critical state for the last three months of the six years leading up to my transplant on July 28, 2000," he said. "During that precarious time, I vowed that if I made it through, I would do everything in my power to help make a difference to the thousands of individuals waiting for a second chance at life. In October 2003, I started the Chris Klug Foundation to promote lifesaving organ and tissue donation and to improve the quality of life for those touched by transplantation."

But transplant or no transplant, this evening was a party. Pop music was pumping over loud speakers at the start line adjacent to the Silver Queen gondola station at the base of Aspen

Mountain. A giant digital clock displayed a countdown to the race start at 5:30 p.m. It was Saturday evening, December 9th, 2017, and it was almost totally dark. Competitors arrived in groups and soon the start area swelled to hundreds of eager racers.

The dress was light ski gear, ski poles, spiked footwear and head lamps. Race numbers were pinned on, and racers with a personal connection to the event wore green stickers denoting either donor family, donor, recipient family, or recipient.

The air was cold, around the freezing mark, and the sky was clear.

"No powder today," Chris lamented over the loudspeaker. As a snowboarder, he lives for snowfalls, preferably heavy and frequent. By contrast, I felt glad that the snow was only on the ground. There was enough to contend with already.

"Five minutes to go before the start of the 2017 Summit for Life!" he announced excitedly.

Competitors dropped off their tagged packs for transport to the top, adjusted lights, took photos, and got ready for the start. At precisely 5:30 p.m. - BOOM! - the gun went off and the race began.

Like everyone, I receive daily emails by the dozen. I must have received the original invitation, but it had probably been lost in the email avalanche of my inbox. The reminder email caught my eye: *Summit for Life.*

> Two Weeks Away!
>
> We are only two weeks away from the 12th Annual Aspen Summit for Life on December 8th & 9th in Aspen, Colorado. Come join us for a weekend celebration of life, featuring a nighttime uphill race on Aspen Mountain benefitting the Chris Klug Foundation. This event will help raise awareness about the importance of organ & tissue donation and living a healthy, active life post-transplant.

I first met Chris Klug a year after my lung transplant. As a new transplant recipient, I was more attuned to events relating to organ donation. He was giving a short speech on the steps of the Capitol Building in Denver to mark "National Donate Life Month", held annually in the month of April.

Chris gave his trademark statement of advocating for increased awareness of organ and tissue donation. "I wouldn't be alive today if it was not for my donor," he declared to a small crowd of assembled families and supporters touched by organ transplant.

Around that time, Chris promoted a general awareness campaign for organ donation on huge highway billboards in Colorado in conjunction with Donor Alliance, the federally-designated organ procurement organization.

My wife Julie had been browsing in a local bookshop one day during my advancing respiratory illness and had come across an ebullient young man sitting at a table signing copies of his book, *To The Edge And Back – My Story from Organ Transplant Survivor to Olympic Snowboarder*. Being an interminable bibliophile, as well as having a husband sitting at home looking down the barrels of a lung transplant, Julie introduced herself and bought a copy. Chris signed one of his books for her and wrote: "Gavin, Enjoy! Best of Luck!"

Like many people with a debilitating health condition, there is a tendency to feel isolated and lonely. Knowing that other people are going through a similar experience is encouraging and inspiring. Chris' book gave me the mental booster shot that I needed to hope for a full recovery. Little did I know that I would be celebrating with him on top of Aspen Mountain a dozen or so years later.

Chris had invited me to join his signature event at least twice before, but I always had an excuse: my children were young, it was close to the holidays, Aspen was far away, the weather was cold, and so on. Besides, hiking two miles up a mountainside in the middle of winter - and at night to boot - sounded dire.

I was always supportive of organ donation awareness, but this was clearly a bridge too far. I don't have a good sense of direction either – put me on an unfamiliar city street and I am sure to head off the wrong way – so the idea of getting lost at night on a mountain in winter was very unappealing. Call me crazy. I let it pass.

I don't know why the email resonated this year, but it did. I checked my calendar to make sure I was free for the upcoming weekend, and wrote a quick email:

---

**From:** Gavin Maitland
**Sent:** Sunday, December 3, 2017 5:31 PM
**To:** Chris Klug
**Subject:** Summit on Sat?

Hi Chris,

I would really like to come up to Aspen this weekend for the summit race. Can I ask you a couple of possibly stupid questions about the race, as I have not done it before?

Is the trail easy to follow with a head light? I don't mind cold, uphill, dark, but I really don't want to get lost.

Thanks so much.
Gavin

---

I received an almost-immediate reply from Chris:

---

**From:** Chris Klug

**Sent:** Monday, December 4, 2017 10:33 AM

**To:** Gavin Maitland

**Subject:** Re: Summit on Sat?

Gavin,

So excited you're thinking about coming to Aspen this weekend for our 12th Annual Aspen Summit for Life. We would

---

absolutely love to have you. It's going to be an awesome weekend. The skiing and snowboarding aren't that epic yet this year, but the uphilling is in perfect shape.

Trail is 2.5 miles, 3,367 vertical up Aspen Mountain. There are two aid stations with ski patrol and a sag wagon at the end if you bonk. There are lanterns every 1/4 mile or so and there should be a stream of about 500 racers in front and behind you. Looks like Saturday night is going to be mild around 46 high and low of 19 degrees, so should be perfect.

I hike in running shoes with microspikes. I recommend using poles as well. I wear light mountaineering pants, and a light first layer and a breathable lightweight jacket, hat, gloves and buff. As long as you keep moving, you don't need much. Most people do it in about 1.5 - 2 hours. You'll be fine. Let me know if you have any other questions or need anything. Keep us posted. So excited to see you again. Thanks, Gavin.

CK

There was only one reply I could make:

**From:** Gavin Maitland
**Sent:** Monday, December 4, 2017 4:05 PM
**To:** Chris Klug
**Subject:** RE: Summit on Sat?

Cool, thanks. I'm in. See you Saturday!

Gavin

Once the race started, everyone surged forward. There were over three hundred competitors that evening pacing or gliding straight up the mountain on the packed snow. The elite athletes surged off at the front, mostly on cross-country skis, as they headed for the summit two-and-a-half miles away. The destination was the post-race party at the summit's Sundeck Restaurant at an altitude of eleven thousand, two hundred feet[39].

Dressing appropriately for this race was tough. The starting air temperature at the base was freezing, but the temperature fell the higher we climbed. Couple that with starting to sweat from the exertion of climbing up a steep ski run, and it became obvious how difficult it was to manage body temperature.

Within the first few minutes, my breathing was deep and rapid. Quite apart from the cold, I could feel the thinness of the Aspen air at eight thousand feet[40]. I was acutely aware that the amount of available oxygen fell with each upward step. Ski poles helped to balance my walking stride and microspikes gave me a sure grip on the packed snow. All I had to do was to put one foot in front of the other and just keep going.

The course was a steep ascent right underneath the gondola. Almost everyone wore a head light strapped to their foreheads, so the snow was visible. If you paused to look up – which took some effort as most of us had our heads focused on the lighted snow directly in front – you could see the stars in the crystal-clear night sky.

There was not a breath of wind. I imagined I could feel the dark masses of trees that lined the track gratefully absorbing our exhaled carbon dioxide as we inhaled their dispelled oxygen.

This was undoubtedly one of my most vigorous lung work-outs, and much more intense than my usual hour of swimming. The exertion demanded a maximum inhalation followed by a maximum exhalation, repeated over and over. I could feel my body shudder as I drew in as much oxygen as I could at each step.

The mechanical Snow Cats were hard at work grinding on one side of the trail and pushing piles of snow to cover bare patches on

---

39  3,400m
40  2,400m

the runs. The snow making machines roared deafeningly at one point on the course as they blasted out compressed air and water into the air to create snow where it was most needed. We could see the snowflakes in the beam of our headlights as we climbed.

At the water stations, small plastic cups of water were handed out. It was like the station at a running race, where runners bunch up as they vie for a cup of water, except this race seemed to be in slow motion. Each competitor accepted a cup of ice cold water before unhurriedly – at least compared to runners - moving on. With a moment of pause, I could turn around and look back down the mountain to enjoy the trail of lights behind me as others made the slow and steady ascent.

Everyone was panting, climbing steadily, and focused on reaching the top. It was a wonderfully positive and enthusiastic atmosphere. I spoke to several fellow competitors. One fellow climber told me how he had received a transplanted heart a year previously. When I asked how he was doing, he replied by gesturing to his chest and said, "I'm doing this!" Fair enough. "Good for you," I said.

The incline suddenly became much steeper. The key was to keep moving. I told myself that the summit was closer with every step. It was like swimming across San Francisco Bay. You just had to keep going. People pay thousands of dollars to come to Aspen to ski down this mountain, I reflected. With three hundred others, I was going the opposite way to raise money, not spend it. I diverted my mind back to the immediate. I had lost feeling in my feet from the cold. So much for warm socks.

The finish came up quickly. Lauren Pierce was at the finish wrapped in a warm coat and congratulating finishers as they crossed the line. A large neon clock displayed my time: one hour, fifty-three minutes. I was happy to have completed the climb in under two hours.

Three hundred and twenty competitors had completed the hike. The fastest male completed it in forty-one minutes, the fastest female in fifty-seven minutes. The oldest female competitor was seventy-one and the oldest male competitor was seventy-five.

The Sundeck Restaurant was only few steps away and the post-race party was already in full swing. The restaurant was packed to the hilt, with a roaring fire and a live band. Most competitors had already arrived, along with family members who had ridden up in the gondola. I filled a plate with hot food, sat down, pulled off my shoes and socks, and held my frozen toes.

Chris held an unpretentious award ceremony to thank tireless fundraisers and contributors to his foundation and the transplant community. The Chris Klug Foundation is one of only a small handful of independent organizations in the country with the reach and wherewithal to organize a fundraiser on this unique and unusual scale. As for Chris, there cannot be many people with the charisma and persuasive ability to convince over three hundred people to hike up a mountain for charity.

In winter.

At night.

For twelve successive years and counting.

Breathtaking.

———————

These are inspiring examples of extraordinary people who are leading the way by giving back. Although generating organ transplant awareness is important, there is of course the other inexorable element: money. While there are many demands for funds, researchers who devote themselves single-mindedly to discovering new treatments deserve special support, in my view.

An integral part of the bridge-to-bridge expeditionary swim was to generate interest and raise funds for lung transplant research. My family and many friends were all involved. Publicized through email and social media and supported by a lot of generosity, we raised $13,000, which we donated to Duke Post-lung Transplant Program.

Duke is one of the largest lung transplant centers in the US. It is the coordinating center for the development of multi-center clinical trials. The grant for the trials will fund the first Lung Transplant Clinical Trials Network, which will include Duke, the Cleveland Clinic, Johns Hopkins University, the University of California – Los Angeles, and the University of Toronto.

The research program is led by my *de facto* partner in health for the last ten years, post-lung transplant pulmonologist, Scott Palmer, MD.

## Scott Palmer, MD

Dr. Palmer's cutting-edge research focuses on several strands of investigation. Firstly, there is genomic and genetic analysis. He asks the tough questions like, "Why do some recipients develop chronic rejection six months after a transplant, while others don't develop it until ten years later, and still others never develop it at all?"

His research is focused on analysis to determine the genetic roots of chronic rejection. His objective is to identify the genetic risk factors that predispose an individual recipient as prone to chronic rejection so early action can be taken.

Secondly, he explores innate immunity. Studies indicate that certain immune system characteristics in some lung transplant recipients trigger an immune response that leads to chronic rejection. More research is needed to determine the specific immune system pathways that lead to chronic rejection and to discover whether existing drugs that target similar responses in patients with conditions such as asthma might also help to prevent chronic rejection.

Thirdly, he wants to understand the links between familial and non-familial idiopathic pulmonary fibrosis (IPF). Dr. Palmer has recently published research that identifies similarities in mutations to related genes in both familial and non-familial IPF. It is believed that further research in tracing this genetic basis of IPF has the potential to lead to earlier and more accurate diagnosis and more effective early interventions.

Fourthly, he wants to develop non-surgical therapies. Most patients with IPF and other advanced lung diseases are not eligible for a lung transplant. Additional research is needed to understand the causes and progression of advanced lung disease to develop advanced non-surgical options for these ineligible patients.

It's a team effort. While a hospital's surgical team gives a patient new lungs and new life, the pre- and post-operative teams deliver personalized care to give each recipient the best chance of a long and successful live after transplant. They are supported by researchers who search for discoveries that will translate into fewer rejections, longer survival times, and richer and fuller lives for lung transplant recipients.

I caught up with Scott Palmer while he was immersed in his lab at Duke. I asked him to describe his "wildest dreams" research break-through for post-lung transplant.

"The best outcomes of our research would be to develop novel and effective means to post-transplant immunosuppression that prevents graft rejection," he said without hesitating. "But at the same time to leave a person's normal immunity intact to fight off infections and free of the many toxicities that occur with current immunosuppression such as kidney toxicity, anemia and other low blood counts.

"In such a world, our lung transplant recipients could expect to enjoy a rich and full life after transplant that is not limited by the development of chronic allograft rejection or bronchiolitis obliterans syndrome (BOS)."

"This sort of breakthrough will come from continued understanding of basic lung immunology and the many ways in which the immune system attempts to target the foreign lung graft," he said.

"As we grow in our understanding of the host immune response specific to the transplant, we also grow in our ability to counter those processes and achieve the goal of improved long-term outcomes."

---

When you are diagnosed with the dark cloud of a life-threatening lung disease, it is hard to see the silver lining. Each of these people accepted a challenge in their own way to give back. Each one inspires me in a different way to swim one more length of the pool or push out boundaries that little bit more to give back to the communities that have given us so much.

Anastasia Darwish speaking for the American Transplant Foundation

Jeff Goldstein, with his wife, Martha Austrich

Olympic medalist and liver transplant recipient, Chris Klug

Scott Palmer, MD. Professor of Medicine, Member in the Duke
Clinical Research Institute, Vice-Chair for Research in the Department
of Medicine, Professor in Immunology, Duke University School of
Medicine, Durham, North Carolina (photo courtesy of Duke University)

# CHAPTER TWELVE: SURVIVAL STORIES

*"When you arrive at a fork in the road, take it."*

- Yogi Berra

## Stories of exceptional physical and mental toughness

The phrase *lies, damned lies, and statistics* is frequently attributed to Mark Twain. It is often used to dull the sharp edges of a data set to avoid it being taken too literally. As statisticians and marketeers the world over are aware, big data is vital, but it can also be massaged into ways that may be misleading.

In the 1970s, it was virtually inescapable that four out of five dentists surveyed recommended sugarless gum for their patients who chewed gum. It wasn't so much saying that sugar-free (read "saccharine-sweetened") was good for you, but that it was preferable to sugar-sweetened gum. In the 1990s NBC comedy, *Friends*, Rachel returned from a job interview, and exclaimed, "Guys! guess what, guess what, guess what!" to which Chandler replied, "Um, ok, the... the fifth dentist caved and now they're all recommending Trident?"

Ask any actuary. Large data sets are useful in making broadly accurate predictions. The company that offers you motor insurance coverage is fairly confident as to the likelihood of you having an accident, based on your age, gender, driving history, where your live, how many miles you drive, and other factors. That's why female drivers are routinely offered lower premiums – data shows that they are less accident-prone than their male counterparts – and why car rental companies steer clear of the under-twenty-fives.

But just because large data sets can make broad generalizations does not necessarily mean they can predict what will happen to you, an individual. If you go to the beach to swim in the ocean, you are much more likely statistically to be killed in a car accident on the drive to the seaside than by a shark once in the water. But your average person has almost no fear about getting into a car, but a huge fear of being attacked by a shark.[41]

But there is no hiding from the fact that the survival statistics for lung transplant are truly awful. Getting knocked around by statistics does not always seem worth it. With a transplant, there is enough to worry about - rejection, infection, and collateral organ damage - without living under the statistical cloud of the "average survivor."

The book *Love, Medicine & Miracles* by Bernie S. Siegel, MD[42], was recommended to me when I was ill. Although he was a practicing surgeon who treated cancer patients, his book contains useful ways of looking at the life of a patient. He writes in an accessible and thought-provoking way. One story centers on a patient who was a professional financial advisor who invested his client's savings based on statistical analysis. The patient was being treated for liver cancer and had been told about his chances of survival by his oncologist. Dr. Siegel recounts how the patient said, "I've spent my life making predictions based on statistics. Statistics tell me I'm supposed to die. If I don't die, my whole life doesn't make sense." The patient went home and died.

Lung transplants have the worst outcomes of all the solid organs. The International Society for Heart & Lung Transplantation is a source of a lot of data. Graphs show survival rates of less than twenty five percent at ten years and less than ten percent at twenty years[43].

My initial intention was to reproduce one of the post-lung transplant survival rate graphs in this book. After looking at the statistics more closely, I found them too depressing. Perhaps they were broad generalizations, but they still could not predict what would happen to one individual. My conclusion? No graphs. Too many lies, damned lies, and statistics. Instead, I prefer to

---

41  Worldwide, approximately one million people on average are killed annually in auto accidents, while less than 10 are killed in reported shark attacks

42  Love, Medicine & Miracles" by Bernie S. Siegel, MD (Harper & Row, Publishers 1986)

43  http://www.ishlt.org/registries/slides.asp?slides=heartLungRegistry

focus on inspiring post-lung transplant stories of determination, perseverance, survival and hope. Here are some of them.

---

Raffaella Bruno-Pinto is Italian and was living in Belgium when she was diagnosed with end-stage lung disease. I received an email from her in 2010, aptly titled "Life."

May 7, 2010

**Subject:** Life

Dear Gavin,

I have just read your book - I actually devoured it - while I was in hospital undergoing all the preliminary tests for a double-lung transplant. Your words made me laugh and cry, but also gave me hope for the future.

In December last year I was diagnosed with non-specific interstitial pulmonitis (NSIP). As I write I am connected to my oxygen extractor, which I use for about 4-5 hours a day for now. It may still be a long while to a transplant. Things are different here in Europe, you have to gain sufficient seniority on the list before it is your turn (sometimes many months).

Undeniably, you, as I, have been blessed with a wonderful and supportive spouse, family and friends, which are all invaluable given the circumstances.

Anyhow I simply wanted to reach out to you and say thank you for writing about your experience. It has helped me as I am sure many others.

Take care.
Raffaella

I stayed in touch with Raffaella after her successful double-lung transplant, and met her, her husband, Michael, and two children, when I visited Brussels two years later. I spoke with her again by phone in February 2018.

Raffaella's symptoms started in 2008 with a dry cough. She consulted several doctors who assumed she had an infection that could be treated with antibiotics. She was continually tired and out of breath. She assumed she was just out of shape, so tried to go to the gym more often. "I would fall asleep reading a book in the afternoon, but I was too embarrassed to tell anyone," she said.

Eventually, she consulted a doctor and pleaded, "Something has to be wrong. We need to do something!"

Her lung function was found to have shrunk to less than half of its predicted level. After many tests and procedures, lung cancer was ruled out, and the cough was attributed to pulmonary fibrosis. She was diagnosed the following year with a rare lung condition called idiopathic nonspecific interstitial pneumonia.

"From what we could find on the internet at the time, the condition only seemed to affect men in their fifties," she recounted. "It said it could be treated with corticosteriods."

Her doctors prescribed a high dose of cortisone, an anti-inflammatory medication. Not only did it not work, it seemed to Raffaella that her condition actually progressed more rapidly.

Post-transplant, she found that there were now two recognized strands of the disease; one cellular and one fibrotic. "The explanations of the disease are different now," she said. "I like to think that perhaps the definition of the disease has changed due to my case."

Generally, the prognosis is better for patients with the cellular form of the disease, which may respond to treatment with anti-inflammatory medication, while the fibrotic disease is irreversible. "Clearly, I had the second strand," she said.

As her health deteriorated, doctors began to consider lung transplant. When her lung function fell below twenty percent and she was on supplementary oxygen twenty-four hours a day, she was admitted to the hospital. In Belgium, the organ procurement process is coordinated by Eurotransplant[44]. Raffaella's doctor submitted an urgent request for lungs. A positive response came back within four hours, she remembered. After that, events moved very quickly.

"I arrived at the hospital on Monday morning," she said. "On Thursday evening, around eleven o'clock, a nurse came into my room and said, "Your lungs are on their way!" The surgeon came to see me and said that the lungs were "magnificent."

Raffaella did not have any contact with the family of her organ donor. "Unfortunately, in Europe, they only accept an anonymous letter," she said. I struggled with this in the beginning. I had what I would call "survivor's guilt" - why did I survive, why did my donor not survive? I struggled with writing a letter to someone who is grieving while I am enjoying a wonderful life."

"Before the transplant, I didn't want to wish for someone to die," she said. "I also struggled with the idea of what if God has decided that this is my time to go. Why am I trying to survive through someone else? But then you can argue that God has decided to send lungs, so you can survive."

Raffaella also met people who were against the concept of organ donation before they knew her story. "They thought it was a case of doctors trying to play God to save people who did not deserve to be saved," she said. One such person lived in Italy and, once she got to know Raffaella better, she changed her mind and registered as an organ donor.

Belgium operates an "opt-out" system for organ donation, which is also being adopted by other countries. For example, the Netherlands also passed an opt-out system into law in 2018, as did France in 2017.

Raffaella also witnessed examples of how increased transplant awareness can also go the other way. She knew of a friend's husband who exercised that right on hearing her

---

44   The Eurotransplant International Foundation, an international non-profit organization responsible for encouraging and coordinating organ transplants in Austria, Belgium, Croatia, Germany, Hungary, Luxembourg, Netherlands, and Slovenia

transplant story and de-registered himself as an organ donor. She says he felt that if he was ever taken to hospital, the doctors would be less willing to save him as they would only see a source of available organs. "I told him that only happens in the movies!" she laughed.

Raffaella attributed her survival as a lung transplant recipient to several factors. "I think mindset, a positive attitude, family and love," she said simply. "I believe that if you believe you can succeed and get your mind connected, it works in your favor. A downward spiral can make things worse. The power of the mind is really important. I feel that I was in the right place at the right time and received the right lungs. And the quality of medical care from my pulmonologist, my surgeon, and the nurses, was first class."

"I don't believe in luck," she went on. "But I do believe in positive thinking. When I was in the hospital, my husband would bring Facebook messages from friends on a printed sheet and read them to me. I was so grateful for all the love, prayers, and positive thoughts. I remember thinking "I can't let everyone down.""

Spreading organ transplant awareness is also important to Raffaella. "I like to tell my story. We are very open about it. I want to show a positive mindset," she said.

The previous October, Raffaella got the chance to do just that. She was invited to speak at the 2017 Eurotransplant Jubilee Congress, which celebrated the organization's fiftieth birthday in the seaside town of Noordwijk in the Netherlands. She gave a ten-minute presentation entitled "Life is a Gift."

The King of the Netherlands, His Majesty King Willem-Alexander, was in the audience. Afterwards, Raffaella and four other organ recipients and donor families sat and chatted with him. The king is an accomplished pilot and had previously served as a reservist in the Royal Netherlands Air Force. Earlier that same year, the media had breathlessly reported that the Dutch king had regularly piloted passenger flights across Europe – always incognito in his KLM uniform - for over twenty years. He had even flown organs for transplant, so was knowledgeable and interested to learn more about the process and asked many questions.

Although many grateful organ recipients may not have known it, their new heart or new lungs, in addition to being the gift of life, may also have been delivered to them personally with a royal seal of approval.

———————————

Ken Douglas received his double-lung transplant in the summer of 2015. The procedure was performed at Toronto General Hospital, well-known as the site of the world's first successful single-lung transplant in 1983 and double-lung transplant in 1986.

Ken was an infantry officer in the British Army and described himself as being very fit prior to his lung disease. He was also a keen rugby player and passionate runner. He initially noticed some wheezing and coughing. As he was still in relatively good health at the time, his condition was not taken seriously by a succession of doctors over several years. Nevertheless, he knew that something was wrong based on his deteriorating physical abilities.

He eventually consulted Professor Paul Corris at Freeman Hospital in Newcastle, UK, who did provide a diagnosis. Ken had a type of idiopathic pulmonary fibrosis, or a scarring of the lungs. Although it cannot be conclusively determined, it is believed that the root cause was likely exposure to unknown contaminants during his deployment during Operation Desert Storm in the Persian Gulf War in 1990-91.

"My transplant was messy," he said. "I waited for two years and it went right down to the wire. I was down to eighteen percent lung capacity. When the surgeons opened me up they found that the scar tissue was much more prevalent than they had previously thought, and it had attached itself to my heart. The heart had literally been pulled across my chest cavity."

The surgeons had the options of either cutting down the size of the donor lungs and transplanting them into his smaller chest cavity or repositioning his heart. They opted for the latter, which caused significant internal bleeding.

"They thought they had lost me on the operating table, but they managed to revive me. The surgery took a lot longer than they'd anticipated," he recounted.

"When I was transferred to the intensive care unit, the complications continued. I was paddled another two times," he said, referring to electric shock defibrillator paddles used for cardiopulmonary resuscitation. "It was touch-and-go, and I was mostly unconscious for the next three weeks," said Ken.

Recovering from the transplant meant addressing the problems associated with significant muscle atrophy. "I was slow coming out of the gate," he said. "But once they got me standing, I was back in my mental comfort zone. It's a different challenge from waiting for the transplant. At the pre-transplant stage, you are training to slow your rate of deterioration. You are working hard, while knowing you are going to get worse. The discipline is not to push yourself harder than necessary, but rather to take your foot off the pedal when you need to. That's a mindset that doesn't come naturally."

He remembered how simply standing was incredibly difficult, as he had been in bed for so long. "The physios were outstanding and determined to get me on my feet as soon as possible. If there was the opportunity to push myself and go a little further, I would take it," he said.

The treadmill held a special challenge for him. He had not run for the past twenty years as his health deteriorated. When he was at his physical peak as an army officer, he could comfortably run over hills with a full pack for hours on end. "That was a breeze compared to the treadmill," he laughed.

"I had put my body through the wringer when I was younger, but I believe that walking on the treadmill after the transplant was physically the hardest thing I have ever done. My legs were dead weight and every step was a monumental effort. It was a great reminder that physical endurance is entirely relative."

It was over a year-and-a-half before he could finally sustain a slow run. His lung capacity had greatly improved but was still only around sixty percent of predicted. He tried exercise patterns of jogging for thirty seconds followed by walking for two minutes, used a stationary bike, and lifted weights. He felt frustrated with little progress as his legs remained stubbornly heavy.

"I have always believed that muscle has memory, but it's not so good long term! I was close to accepting that perhaps running would never be an option for me."

He received advice to simply listen to his body. Once he felt the need to walk, he walked. He tried exercise methods such as "Couch to 5k" which is aimed at people who have never been runners.

"I also read an article on "slow jogging" by Dr. Tanaka, a Professor at Fukuoka University, which has helped a lot of older people," he said. "It's low impact and even slower than walking. It sounds overly simplistic, but that's what I did," he said.

"The fact that it was jogging, even though it was slower than I could walk, helped me psychologically. In my mind, once I was jogging, it was merely a matter of building up the pace. I stuck with it and it served me well. I ran the Ottawa "10k" in eighty minutes in May 2017 with my eldest son. From surgery to running ten kilometers took me almost exactly two years."

The ten-kilometer run generated media coverage in Canada which Ken used to highlight the importance of organ donation. Afterwards, he felt that although it had served a good purpose, running races was probably not the right route for him. Psychologically, it had been hugely important, but he decided to switch his focus to less jarring activities.

"I'm not going to push for a half or a full marathon," said Ken. "I've moved to resistance training with weights. I had been sedentary for so long and much of my body had wasted away, so I spent time to make it stronger. I'm enjoying getting strength back with compound exercises that use the bigger muscle groups, such as dead-lifts, bench-presses and pull-ups, which are sufficiently aerobic for me. I also do a lot of stretching to help with my posture."

"My lung capacity is up to almost seventy percent, and I'm told that's as high as it will go, although I'm determined to nudge it a little higher. The occasional infection and the anti-rejection drugs slow my progress but, the more that I do, the lighter my legs get and generally the easier and more natural the movement feels."

Ken continually reminds himself what his body has been through and marvels at what it is capable of. "I love being outdoors and active. I'm looking forward to getting into cross-country skiing," he said. "I tried swimming, but I got an infection and ended up in the ICU briefly. Swimming is not my thing. I prefer walking and jogging for the pure joy of it."

As far as the role of psychological strength in his recovery, "I think I have always been reasonably robust," he said. "Physical endurance comes from mental determination. You can't get one without the other. You have to want it, and I'm a big believer in taking your motivation from wherever you find it. But as a transplant recipient, you also have to be patient."

"When you get an infection, you have to stop or reduce your exercise, let the infection clear, knowing that you'll lose ground, and then start again. I often pause, take in a deep breath and am thankful for the air, the day, walking around, and getting to live my life with my wife and sons."

---

Duke helped to connect me with another recipient who had graduated from the lung transplant program a few months before I arrived in 2008. We were similar in age and shared the distinction of not being in the COPD, cystic fibrosis or IPF disease categories – we were in the odd lung disease category of "other".

James was a doctor from London who went through a similar jarring experience of being turned down by a hospital as "inoperable." I valued his unique perspective on the convergence of the body's physiology and physical exercising for recovery in this post-transplant world that we both inhabited. Once we were in touch, we exchanged emails and phone calls.

"I went from being a serious cross-country runner to wheelchair bound on continuous oxygen in the space of three years," he said.

"I was thirty when I was diagnosed out of the blue with pulmonary hypertension. The family doctor failed to diagnose it at all and, in the end, I did all my own tests when I was on call at the hospital where I worked and took them to a cardiologist. From then on it was all downhill. Over the next three years I got progressively worse and ended up unable to walk, with severe respiratory and cardiac failure," he said.

"I was on the UK transplant list but was unlikely to get a transplant due to the length of wait and the fact I was too sick to tolerate the operation," he said.

Via a serendipitous route, he ended up at Duke Hospital in the United States as a candidate for a double-lung transplant.

As a medical doctor, James had a unique perspective on physical exercise. "Exercise is interesting," he explained. "For the first two years after my transplant, I did loads of running and did get quite fit. On the treadmill I could run for twenty minutes at twelve kilometers per hour quite comfortably. Now I do half this."

James often questioned why he had not been able to return to his pre-illness fitness levels. He arranged for additional lung tests and bronchoscopy, but found that the results were "normal," at least for a lung transplant person. He rued his overall lack of fitness. "Being on steroids, you lose fitness rapidly," he said. "Steroids also inhibit muscle build up and generally do not help." (Prednisone is a catabolic steroid, the opposite to the anabolic steroid that some athletes may use illegally).

"Also, the transplanted lungs will never be so good. There will be microscopic damage across their structure and the anastomosis (a surgical connection between adjacent blood vessels) where they are stitched in, which causes airway narrowing.

"Lung transplants never seem to do as well as the other organ transplants in regaining fitness," he concluded.

---

I re-connected with Scott Johnson from North Carolina in mid-February 2018. Scott was diagnosed with cystic fibrosis when he was two months old and received a double-lung transplant when he was twenty-nine.

Scott and his wife Leanne were featured in a 2011 book[45] which followed the progress of six amateur athletes preparing for an Ironman triathlon. The event has been referred to, not entirely unfairly, as the collective athletic insanity of a 2.4-mile open-water swim, a 112-mile bike ride and a 26.2-mile marathon run.

He described the achievements of which he was most proud of in his post-transplant life. I expected his focus would be on his Herculean athletic achievements and thought he had competed in five Ironman triathlons.

"I've actually done seven," he said, correcting me. "I'm retired now," he laughed. He didn't need to think for long before expanding. "I'm most proud of meeting the girl of my dreams and being married for ten years," he replied, referring to his wife, Leanne. "I could not have met her and got married if it was not for my lung transplant."

Quite apart from the usual drama that surrounds a lung transplant, Scott's experience contained a remarkable twist. Lungs became available in the fall of 2001 but, as he was being prepared for the transplant operation at the University of North Carolina, the tragic events of September 11th occurred. Air traffic in the United States was immediately grounded. The lungs could not reach him.

"I didn't get my lungs on September 11th," he recalled. "The doctors thought it was the signing of my death warrant. But I did get lungs on September 15th. That was my day. It's what I consider my second birthday. I don't know what happened with those first lungs. I hope they went to somebody who needed them."

He explained his attitude and overall philosophy towards exercising after a lung transplant. "Post-transplant, I would expect that most people would go crazy with exercise, but it seems not to be the case," he said. "My overall thinking is that if you couldn't run prior to a lung transplant, why wouldn't you want to run a marathon with new lungs? That's the way I think. When I got my lung transplant, some people were telling me, "accept the gift you've been given and relax. Live your life.""

45 "You Are an Ironman: How Six Weekend Warriors Chased Their Dream of Finishing the World's Toughest Triathlon" by Jacques Steinberg (Viking, 2011)

"In my opinion, living my life meant pushing the boundaries of what I had been given and not just sitting on the couch. That's what I identify with. If you couldn't do something before and, suddenly, you are given a second chance at life, you need to make the most of it. I hope that the transplant people I have met are taking advantage of their gift."

I knew Scott liked to swim, with swimming being one of the three triathlon disciplines. I found swimming to be an easier post-transplant endurance sport than running. With swimming, I could still be competitive among my peers but, with running, I was in the lowest ten percent of any group.

"I'm the same," he agreed. "I think that lung-transplant people are at a running disadvantage. I have talked to a lot of people who have had transplants and many of them say they have an issue with running. I thought it was just me."

"I spoke to a former US Navy Seal who was having the same issues. I think that throughout the whole process, the nerves that interact with the rest of the body are cut – something doctors have not identified yet. I can swim like a fish and I can bike. But running kills me every time."

In terms of advice to someone who was heading towards a lung transplant, he said, "I would tell them to be as active as they can and as physically fit as possible."

It is over sixteen years since his transplant operation. Sixteen years seems a monumental achievement, but Scott commented that he lives within a few miles of the first double-lung recipient in the south-east of the United States who is twenty-two years out. I asked Scott to what he attributed his success - and added that I was touching my wooden desk again.

"Making sure you take the medications is number one on the priority list, outside everything else we have talked about," he said. "Before my transplant, I worked in data management with pharmaceutical testing. I was always a numbers and process person. I don't have an agenda for every day, but it always involves taking my medications and being on time." His disciplined background undoubtedly helps compliance.

Staying active and physically fit is also vital. And perhaps so is an element of individuality and toughness of spirit.

"I didn't realize the average survival time for lung transplant recipients until after the fact," he laughed. "I didn't know the boundaries. So being physically fit and always pushing boundaries," he said. "And not thinking inside the box."

I don't think anyone could accuse him of that.

———————

I was starkly reminded about how nothing can be taken for granted when I spoke to James Watson, a cystic fibrosis patient who received a double-lung transplant almost thirteen years before. I asked him how physical exercise helped his post-transplant recovery.

"After my transplant, I was back playing hockey within six months. I competed in four Transplant Games[46] in basketball, volley ball, track and field, golf, bowling, and racket ball. In the Winter Games, I participated in snowboarding and curling. I still stay as active as possible, although in the past three years, I've been busy having a baby, a dog, and working more."

James had enjoyed good health for most of his first eleven post-transplant years. In the last couple of years, his pulmonary function tests (PFTs) have declined due to a build-up of scar tissue in his lungs, linked to chronic rejection.

"Around the time of New Years, I caught a virus which made my PFTs drop way down." I asked him what he mean by "way down?" PFTs, or spirometry tests, are usually gauged against a predicted one hundred percent.

"Around seventeen percent," he said.

He explained that he is being treated at the University of Colorado Hospital in Denver and, about a year before, his transplant doctors put him on night-time supplementary oxygen. Because of his recent drop in lung function, he is now back on oxygen twenty-four hours a day. The severity of his lung condition qualifies him to be listed for a second double-lung transplant.

———————

46  www.transplantgamesofamerica.org

"I was told I am number one on the transplant list as of last Thursday," he said.

Although the prospect of the protracted ordeal of a second lung transplant was daunting, James had a pragmatic attitude. "I just want to get it done," he said. "Walking around like this is tiring. It's not who I am. I want to get the time back with my little guy." James' son is eighteen months old. "I want to ice skate with him," he said.

"I am relieved and happy that I have been approved to get another transplant. It is not always done. I think the doctors figure that I am someone who did not waste the first transplant – I got thirteen years from it – and I did many things, including travelling the world."

Since his lung transplant, James has participated in the World Transplant Games in Finland, and has visited Scotland, Italy, and was married in Jamaica.

"I have a positive attitude," he said. "Being approved again is really a blessing. I don't like having to be – as it means I got sick – but being approved makes me very happy. This time around I have a lot more knowledge about what to expect."

James' motivation is strong, and he explained what keeps him going. "You've got to live every day," he said. "Enjoy every breath you get. The last thirteen years have been the best years of my life. I met my wife, I've taken trips around the world, and my son was born."

James' son's birthday was his eleven-year transplant anniversary. "That will always be the most special day ever because I got two miracles on the same day, eleven years apart," he said. "I have done so many things and made so many new friends, it's been worth it. Right now, it kinda sucks, but it has been worth every scar and every pill I have had to take.

"I experienced thirteen more years of life and I still have a lot more to go," he said. "If anyone asks me if they should have a transplant, I tell them that it is trading one serious condition for another one. But if you're tough enough, have the mental stability, want to live and enjoy life, it is the way to go."

---

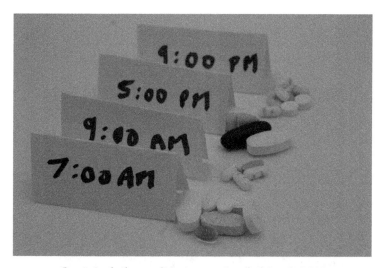

Gavin's daily medication regimen. March 2018

Early outdoor morning swimming at Colorado Athletic Club in Boulder.
March 2018 (photo by Scott Coe)

Gavin at Chris Klug Foundation's Summit for Life.
December 2017

Raffaella Bruno-Pinto

Lachlan and Jock with Ken Douglas competing in the
Ottawa Race Weekend 10km road race.
May 2017 (photo: Jack Burkom)

# CHAPTER THIRTEEN: EXERCISE & LUNG TRANSPLANT

*"I have always believed exercise is a key not only to physical health but to peace of mind. Many times in the old days I unleashed my anger and frustration on a punch bag rather than taking it out on a comrade or even a policeman. Exercise dissipates tension, and tension is the enemy of serenity. I found that I worked better and thought more clearly when I was in good physical condition, and so training became one of the inflexible disciplines of my life."*
- Nelson Mandela, Long Walk to Freedom

*"The next time I see a jogger smiling, I'll consider it."*
- Joan Rivers, on physical exercise

## Thumbs up for exercise

For the general population, physical exercise is probably good for you. The American Heart Association recommends forty minutes of aerobic exercise three to four times a week. The US government advises that "adults who are active are healthier and less likely to develop chronic diseases than adults who aren't active."

General advice suggests that any amount of physical exercise has health benefits and any physical activity is better than none. Weekly recommendations include two-and-a-half hours of aerobic activity, such as walking or tennis, as well as two or more days of muscle-strengthening activities, such as lifting weights or using resistance bands.[47]

Although there are many anecdotes about the benefit of exercise to post-lung transplant recipients, it's hard to prove. Evidence-based medicine relies upon studies to demonstrate if a therapy or medication works. I wanted to review scientific evidence and determine how, if at all, I could relate back to my own experience of physical exercise.

---

47  www.health.gov

Doctors and medical researchers evaluate how a sample of patients do in response to a specific treatment (e.g. a surgery, a medication, or a type of treatment). Sometimes, they review data from the past (retrospective study) or the future (prospective study) which allows them to measure the response of a specific treatment against a control group.

It's the comparison which allows meaningful conclusions to be drawn, as well as a having a large enough population sample. Anecdotal evidence ("I heard about a guy who...") is generally dismissed by the medical profession as irrelevant.

The challenge with lung transplant recipients is that the population size is small and lung recipients have come from many different disease origins. That makes it difficult to find a sample that is large or representative enough to draw any meaningful conclusions. The main diseases that may lead to a lung transplant, such as COPD, pulmonary fibrosis and cystic fibrosis, all have wildly different disease profiles.

Clinical research studies generally use a population sample as a basis of study. The larger the sample size, the more reliable the conclusions. For example, if a pharmaceutical company is studying the effectiveness of its new cholesterol-lowering drug, a sample size of 4,000 patients is better than a sample size of twenty (sample size is referred to as the letter "n" so, in this example, n = 4,000).

**Studies on physical exercise & transplant**

With all these caveats and difficulties, it is still useful to ask what do the experts and published scientific studies say. Entirely appropriately, the weight of scientific study has focused on the two most critical periods for lung transplant: the pre-transplant phase and the post-transplant phase (immediately after discharge from the hospital and up to about one year).

To see if I could obtain any broad conclusions, I reviewed a non-exhaustive selection of some of the most recent studies. For example, a scientific article in 2017[48] examined pulmonary

---

48   Schneeberger T, et al. Respiration. 2017:94(2): 178-185

rehabilitation outcomes after single or double-lung transplant for 722 patients from 1997 to 2016 with COPD or interstitial lung disease. The goal was to compare differences in outcomes between these recipients through performance on a six-minute walk using retrospective data. Although the study concluded that "all benefitted significantly" regarding exercise capacity, and that no differences were found between single and double-lung transplant, the study only went out to one-year post-transplant. The authors acknowledge that outcome data is limited with respect to the lung transplant population.

Another 2016 study[49] looked to see if there was any consistent measurement of outcomes in physical activity of all solid organ transplant recipients. The authors retrieved and reviewed over four hundred scientific articles that looked at the effect of exercise training in solid organ transplant recipients. (Incidentally, only three lung transplant recipients were found). The study concluded that there is little standardization of trials relating to exercise involving solid organ transplant recipients, which limits any conclusions.

A study in 2016[50] considered perceived barriers and facilitators to physical activity in organ transplant recipients. The study noted that physical activity is important for organ transplant recipients, but many recipients did not meet the recommended amount or type of exercise.

A 2017 podcast[51] on the American Thoracic Society's website provided some well-founded information on lung transplant rehabilitation. The challenges of measuring data and drawing any meaningful conclusions are evident, even when they are focused on outpatient and closely monitored rehabilitation activities. Two pulmonary specialists from Canada were interviewed, Lisa Wickerson, BScPT, MSc, PhD(c), a physical therapist at the Toronto Lung Transplant Program, University Health Network,

---

49  Janaudis-Ferreira T, et al. World J Transplant 2016. Dec 24;6(4): 774-789

50  van Adrichem EJ, et al. PLoS One. 2016 Sep 13;19(11(9)

51  https://www.thoracic.org/about/ats-podcasts/lung-transplant-rehabilitation.php . Accessed 3/13/2018

and Sunita Mathur, PT, PhD, an assistant professor at the University of Toronto.

Lisa Wickerson described how the University Health Network is a large program - one of the largest in the world - which performed over 140 adult lung transplant surgeries in 2016. The podcast looked at several areas relating to physical exercise and solid organ transplant, including lung transplant. In terms of supporting evidence, the field of exercise during the post-transplant phase is still in its infancy. For example, what is the appropriate length of time for post-transplant rehabilitation?

Ms. Wickerson referred to a 2017 study by Fuller et al[52] which looked at the effects of a supervised post-lung transplant rehabilitation program over seven and fourteen weeks. The study concluded that there were comparable improvements between the two groups.

"Program duration is only one aspect of rehabilitation," she said. "We also need to evaluate the frequency, intensity, duration and modes of training."

Her colleague, Dr. Mathur, commented that there are some opportunities for transplant recipients to participate in sports, high performance, and endurance activities; therefore, sporting goals such as Transplant Games are important.

Dr. Mathur described the two main physiological limitations to physical exercise post-transplant. Firstly, central limitations, which refer to the heart and lungs. Secondly, peripheral limitations refer to the circulation and muscle.

"After a lung transplant, the central limitation, which was the main limiting factor of impaired ventilation, is alleviated. However, exercise capacity still does not reach predicted levels in most transplant recipients," she said. "Studies from the 1990s showed that, on average, lung transplant recipients reached about forty to sixty percent of predicted VO2max,[53] or aerobic

---

52  Fuller LM, et al. Arch Phys Med Rehabil. 2017;98(2):220-226

53  VO2max is the maximum oxygen uptake and refers to the amount of oxygen a body is capable of using in one minute. It is a measure of capacity for aerobic work

capacity. This is similar across other transplant groups, such as heart, kidney and liver."

She continued, "The focus of exercise capacity post-transplant is mostly on peripheral limitations, and primarily on the muscles' ability to extract and utilize oxygen. This ability seems to be impaired post-transplant and it might be related to de-conditioning and to the immunosuppressant medications."

## Broad recommendations

Based on the scientific evidence, it is fair to ask about broad recommendations for exercise for people undergoing lung transplant.

"The major component is aerobic training and resistance training for stable and uncomplicated post-transplant patients," continued Ms. Wickerson in the same podcast interview. "Aerobic training like treadmill work and cycling can be started at a moderate intensity, around sixty percent on a cycle or seventy-five to eighty percent of maximum from a six-minute-walk test results.

She also noted that there are few specific evidence-based guidelines for resistance training for any of the solid organ groups, so there are no clear guidelines on the best approaches for training, and whether strength or endurance-based training should be emphasized. Based on current research and their own clinical experience, approaches to exercise are summarized in an expert review[54], which covers aerobic and resistance training for post-lung transplant recipients.

It is interesting to note that in many studies, the phrase "long-term" is used for anything around one-year post-transplant. The focus of the majority of lung transplant exercise studies is on the pre-transplant period, or in the immediate post-transplant period, up to one year out. Post-transplant, studies have been limited to a highly-monitored environment, with evaluations such as the six-minute-walk test. If one-year post-transplant is considered long-term, what is ten years? What is twenty years?

---

54   Wickerson, et al. World J Transplant 2016; 6(3): 517-531

To expand on these questions, I spoke with Ms. Wickerson by phone in mid-March 2018 and asked her if she was aware of any additional studies that looked at the benefits of physical exercise following a post-lung transplant for long-term recipients.

"There are side-effects of the medications and a lot of conditions that people can develop long-term, like issues with kidneys or high blood pressure," Ms. Wickerson said. "Exercise has been shown to benefit some chronic conditions, for example, if someone has developed diabetes or hypertension."

A study by Langer[55] looked at physical activity by studying people early on, then one-year post-transplant. The people who exercised had lower blood pressure than those who didn't. "That's an important outcome," she said.

Ms. Wickerson also commented that it had been thought there would be physical exercise limitations because of the transplanted lungs or heart, but that wasn't the case. The limitation was actually in the muscles. Some of the medications that are very important after a transplant, like prednisone and tacrolimus, affect muscles so they might not be able to extract oxygen from blood and use it as effectively as without those medications. Lung function may be a hundred percent, which is good, but that is not where the limitation lies. "At the muscle level, even if the blood with the oxygen gets there, the muscle itself isn't as effective," she said. "We don't know enough about it."

A study by Painter, an exercise physiologist, reviewed transplant recipients competing in a US Transplant Games[56]. The study found that peak fitness was a lot higher than the forty to sixty percent mentioned earlier. This group was performing at a much higher level than non-exercising lung transplant recipients.

A two-day meeting was held in Toronto in 2013 where experts and contributors convened from many areas of solid organ transplant: clinicians, researchers, administrators, and patients to look at research priorities and an agenda for exercise[57]. The authors of the paper acknowledged that "there is limited

55   Langer D. Respiration 2015; 89(5): 353-62
56   Painter P, et al. Transplantation. 1997;64(12):1795-800
57   Mathur S, at al. Am J Transplant. 2014;14(10):2235-45

research supporting the benefits of exercise training, particularly for long-term benefits and outcomes beyond exercise capability and quality of life."

As a ten-year-out post-lung transplant recipient, my physical exercise questions are centered more around performance over a six-mile swim or thirteen-mile run, as opposed to a six-minute walk. Given the paucity of hard evidence, some "out-of-the-box" thinking is undoubtedly required.

## Limeys

James Lind (1716–1794) was a Scottish physician and surgeon who served with the British Royal Navy and applied some "out-of-the-box" thinking to solving a serious problem of the day. He carried out experiments to discover the cause of scurvy, the debilitating disease which we now know was caused by vitamin C deficiency. Scurvy was a common condition among poorly nourished sailors at the time, with symptoms including bleeding gums, poor wound healing, and eventual death.

Dr. Lind found that sailors given oranges, lemons and limes experienced a rapid recovery. He is credited with definitively establishing the health benefits of citrus fruits, although he probably did not fully understand why they worked. Once implemented, the incidence of scurvy fell to almost zero. Why is Dr. Lind relevant to lung transplant?

I believe he provides an example of finding and applying a treatment without concrete scientific evidence. It seems intuitive that exercise and physical activity are beneficial to post-lung transplant recipients even without the support of evidence-based data. In some circumstances, anecdotal evidence may be better than no evidence at all.

## Mount Kilimanjaro

Sometimes doctors and transplant recipients team up to push the boundaries and generate their own scientific evidence. In 2015, the Groningen Transplant Center in the Netherlands organized an ascent of Mount Kilimanjaro, Africa's highest peak. The group was comprised of twelve organ transplant recipients, eight of whom reached the summit[58]. Two lung transplant recipients were in the group of intrepid climbers. The researchers concluded that the tolerance of the transplanted recipients to physical activity in a high-altitude expedition was comparable to non-transplanted peers.

In 2017, Peter Jaksch, head of the lung transplant program at the Medical University of Vienna, coordinated another ascent of Mount Kilimanjaro, with eight lung transplant volunteers from across Europe.

The results were also equally amazing. After training for six months, the group succeeded in climbing the 19,431[59] feet peak with breathing test results that showed they actually had better lung functionality than some of the doctors who made the ascent with them.

"That feeling when you stand at the top and you can look around and see what you have done – that is the best feeling," said one of the climbers, forty-two-year-old Helmut Steigersdorfer, who had a lung transplant in 2002 due to cystic fibrosis.[60]

## Mind, body & breathing

Emma Willox is a Melbourne-based personal trainer and pilates instructor. I asked her which activities she would recommend beyond aerobic and resistance training that may be beneficial for post-lung transplant.

"The connection between the mind and body is very important," she said. "Any movement that connects the mind to the body will help release tension. This also helps with releasing tightness in the body and stretching out the fascia - the fibrous connective tissue beneath the skin that wraps around every bone and joint - thus allowing the muscles to get a deeper stretch."

She went on to say how muscle tightness is the enemy of flexibility, which in turn affects aerobic ability. "For example,

---

58   van Adrichem EJ, et al. 2015 PLOS ONE:10.1371. Nov 25 2015
59   5,895 m
60   Source: www.thetimes.co.uk/article/lung-transpalnt-patients-conquer-kilimanjaro: 8/7/2017. Accessed 3/7/2018

tight hip flexors will affect your range of motion, ranging from poor squat technique to a poor posture when running," she said. "Flexibility can start as easily as using a simple breathing technique to expand the rib cage."

"Inhale and really visualize the diaphragm blowing up like a balloon, while pushing the rib cage out at the front, back and sides," Emma suggested.

## Yoga poses

I sat down with Kimi Tasker in December 2017 to ask about her yoga philosophy. Kimi is an effusive New Zealander who teaches yoga at an idyllic retreat on the south coast of Nicaragua. On her journey to Central America, she has taught yoga for over twenty years in six countries across four continents.

I joined her yoga class by the beach and found it more accessible than previous classes I had attempted. I had generally chosen a yoga class based on the day and time it was being held, as opposed to seeking out a particular type. Kimi's classes focused on finding and maintaining stretches, without feeling rushed to move from one pose to the next. I could feel the benefit of the flexibility training in building on aerobic and resistance training.

I was understandably interested in breath. The word I hear frequently as an occasional yoga practitioner was *prana*. What was the importance of *prana*?

"All types of yoga fall under an umbrella of *hatha*", she said. *Ha* is breath and *atha* is now. All yoga is *hatha*, so it's really breathing in the now. And *prana* is the concept of using the *hatha* to cultivate life energy. *Prana* is the experience of breath. It is the drawing of the breath from the earth, through the body, the lungs, the spine, and the crown of the head, to connect with something that keeps breath flowing. And the *prana* is like a circular form of energy. *Prana*'s translation is "life force energy."

"In order to control and engage the breath," she went on "we have a concept called *pranayama*. So *prana* is the life force energy and *yama* is to engage it. And *pranayama* is a really big part of the practice of yoga. It's about moving your breath

194

through your body to bring it to parts of your body which may need healing. There are a lot of exercises that you do to engage the breath. The simple act of doing the *asana* is that it invites you to use *pranayama*, where you shift the breath through your body. Yoga teaches you to engage your breath," said Kimi.

It's more of an intuitive link between the kind of muscle flexibility training that yoga provides and the more established benefits of aerobic and resistance training. For example, in 2015, the Australian Government's Department of Health published the results of a review of alternative therapies that sought to determine if any were suitable for health insurance coverage. Yoga was one of the practices evaluated for which no clear evidence of effectiveness was found. But as Dr. Lind discovered, just because there is no evidence-based data does not mean an activity is not beneficial.

In theory, yoga still sounded like exactly like the post-lung transplant type of exercise I should be doing. In practice, I can honestly say that I did not exactly love it, but I did love how it made me feel. I still have a lot to learn and recognize that I am still a yoga work-in-process. Perhaps that's why they call it "practice?"

## Finding beneficial activities

For my part, my physical exercise activities are built on the post-transplant rehabilitation base to extend to aerobic swimming and running, weight training and resistance work, as well as flexibility activities, mostly carried out at altitude.

As an aside, I have often wondered why my post-lung transplant swimming ability is better than my running ability. Comparing myself to a group of able-bodied peers, I am reasonably competitive in the pool, but not on the running track. Based on reviewed post-lung transplant scientific evidence, frowned-upon anecdotal evidence, and a sample size of n = 1 (just me), here is my theory of why my swimming ability is better than running:

In *running*, you are technically working all your leg muscles during each run, but some more than others. Everyone is slightly different, but generally you would use calf, hamstrings and quad muscles[61]. In *swimming*, by contrast, you use twenty-four muscles[62] on each side of your body, so you use forty-eight muscles on each freestyle stroke to move through the water. Some of the muscles are used when pulling, some when kicking, some when rotating your body, some when breathing, and some extra muscles when doing flip turns.

Given the medial explanation of the impact of immunosuppressant medications on muscles and their impaired ability to effectively use oxygen, my hypothesis is that the negative impact is spread over a much larger area, so is dissipated more widely, where a larger muscle group is used (i.e. in swimming). That is my hypothesis of why swimming is easier than running in my post-transplant immunocompromised state.

Assuming this explanation has some validity, what do you do to maintain optimal health while taking long-term immunosuppressants? The answer must be a regular blend of aerobic, strength training and flexibility training to include as many large muscle groups as possible, all reviewed and approved by a doctor. All-body workouts that may work especially well for lung transplant recipients may include activities such as cross-country skiing, rock climbing, cross-fit and yoga.

Up to 2017, I felt too intimidated to join a running group, despite my long-held beliefs about the positive motivational effects of group exercising. In my experience, running groups are usually made up of dedicated runners who relentlessly notch up dozens of miles a week. Although I used to be a runner pre-transplant, I felt that my running ability was weak. At the same time, I knew that the only way to get through a fear was to face it head on.

Determined to up my running game in time for the *Team Transplant* half-marathon in the fall 2017, I joined a running group called Boulder Striders. The sessions were led by professional running and triathlete coaches, Darren and Colleen De Reuck.

---

61  www.cari-fit.com/2011/11/what-muscles-do-i-use-when-i-run/ Accessed 3/15/2018

62  http://chrismannswimcoach.blogspot.com/2012/03/what-muscles-do-i-use-when-i-swim.html. Accessed 3/15/2018

When I got back from my first running training session in over twenty years, I felt tired, but cheerful. I had made a big step – or stride – forward in my exercising regimen.

Julie was more skeptical.

"Were you just running up and down?" The very idea of running was anathema to her.

"No, we were doing running drills. Fast and slow," I said. "It's good fun. It's called Fartlek."

"What?" Riley sniggered.

"Fartlek," I repeated. "It's a type of training."

"That's not a word," Riley said accusatorially. "You're making that up!"

"I'm not," I assured her. "It's a real thing."

She grabbed her phone and rapidly punched her fingers at the tiny screen. What would have taken several hours of arguing two decades before took her only a few seconds now. "Oh, you're right," she conceded, almost disappointedly. She read from her phone. "Fartlek means "speed play" in Swedish where faster running is mixed with slower running."

"It's just interval training," she concluded with a shrug.

"I guess, yes."

Happily, the terminology did not affect the experience. While I kept running, I realized that I will probably not regain pre-lung-transplant running abilities. I have always liked the imagery of making my transplanted lungs feel "at home" in my body through cardiovascular exercise. What better way for them to feel at home than to be exercised and appreciated every day?

That does not mean that I cannot enjoy running for the sheer cardiovascular joy of it and accept that I am probably a regular at the back of the pack.

I think I can live with that.

# CHAPTER FOURTEEN: SWIMMING THROUGH ADVERSITY

*"What seems to us as bitter trials are often blessings in disguise."*

- Oscar Wilde

## Just keep going

Resilience in the face of adversity is fascinating. It is a recurring theme for historical figures such as George Washington, Abraham Lincoln, Franklin D. Roosevelt, Gandhi, Martin Luther King, Winston Churchill, and Nelson Mandela. How many of these historical giants would you have even heard of if it was not for the adversity they faced?

At some point in life, almost all of us will have to go through some bad patches. Challenges come in many forms: physical threats such as relationships, health or financial challenges, or psychological threats, such as frustration and unfulfilled goals. There is no teacher like adversity. You can learn a lot from the hard times. Look around and see numerous individuals who have set precedents by their extraordinary resilience and tenacity in the face of troubles. People like Helen Keller and Stephen Hawking are constant sources of inspiration. Adversity can be a powerful force.

Bear Grylls, former special forces soldier turned host of the NBC adventure series, *Man vs Wild*, knows a thing or two about adversity. He summited Mount Everest when he was twenty-three, eighteen months after breaking his back jumping out of an airplane.

"Whether I have been in the middle of a dusty, barren desert, stuck in a mosquito-infested swamp, or freezing cold and wet, there is always one thing I tell myself above everything else – and it is an easy one to remember, even when you are dog-tired and not feeling particularly brave. It is this…just keep going," he wrote.[63]

---

63  "A Survival Guide for Life": Bear Grylls (2012)

As a swimmer, I am awed by stories of epic survival, especially in cold water. An article in the British Medical Journal[64] recounted how a twenty-three-year-old Icelandic fisherman swam three miles to the safety of shore in forty-one degree[65] water. The swim took up to six hours. Most people immersed in water colder than forty-three degrees usually die of hypothermia within seventy-five minutes.

When the fishing boat capsized, the fisherman and two co-workers initially climbed onto the boat's keel but, after forty-five minutes, decided to attempt to swim for shore three miles away. After ten minutes, both companions disappeared, presumed drowned. The twenty-three-year old carried on and eventually reached shore.

Researchers tried to determine what attributes allowed him to survive the cold-water immersion when his co-workers did not. They found that his surprising survival could only be partly-attributed to the thickness of his subcutaneous fat. It may have been that "just keep going" thing which took him the rest of the way.

The psychologist Al Siebert (1934-2009) became interested in the personalities of survivors. Dr. Siebert was the founder and director of The Resiliency Center, a former army paratrooper in the Korean War and taught management psychology for over forty years at Portland State University. He became internationally recognized for his pioneering research into psychological resilience and the inner nature of highly resilient survivors. He interviewed hundreds of people who had lived through all kinds of hardships and authored several books on resilience and survivor traits, including best-seller, *The Resiliency Advantage*.

Dr. Siebert found that one of the most prominent characteristics of survivors is a certain complexity of character. He found that survivors were both serious and playful, tough and gentle, logical and intuitive, hard-working and lazy, aggressive and shy, introspective and outgoing, and so on.

64  BMJ 292:18 Jan 1986 171-172
65  5°C

199

Survivors were people who did not fit into neat categories. As a result, it made them more flexible than many other people in difficult circumstances, as they had a wider array of resources to draw upon to get through adversity.

One of those survivors may well be former Miami Dolphins fullback, Rob Konrad. He fell off his small boat in 2015[66] while fishing alone nine miles from land. He swam for sixteen hours towards shore lights and reached Palm Beach at 4:30 a.m. the next morning, some twenty-seven miles away. His feat was a demonstration of athleticism and unbelievable willpower. "Five or six hours in, I realized that maybe I can do this," he said afterwards.

Diana Nyad, the endurance swimmer, commented, "Taking his life in his hands and deciding to save himself. It's an incredible story."

In some cases when your boat capsizes, or you fall overboard, there is no other option than to swim for it. In other cases, the swim for survival is voluntary. In 2015, New Zealand-native, thirty-eight-year-old Kim Chambers swam thirty miles from the Farallon Islands in the Pacific back to San Francisco in just over seventeen hours. While more than 4,000 people have conquered Mount Everest, she is only the fifth person – and the first woman – to conquer the Farallon Islands swim.

Her achievement is remarkable for several reasons. The swim is one of the most challenging in the world due to cold water, strong winds and waves, not to mention one of the world's largest clusters of great white sharks. But more than that, she had only been swimming seriously for four years before she emerged as one of the world's most accomplished marathon swimmers.

But here is the most remarkable part. A seemingly inconsequential accident - she slipped on a staircase at age seventeen - badly injured her leg. The trauma left her crippled with an estimated one percent chance of ever walking on her own again. After years in physical therapy, she took to the water to exercise and recover. One of her first open-water swims was the Alcatraz swim, and she progressed to completing the Oceans

---

66  Reported by *The Associated Press* Jan 12, 2015

Seven, which is the long-distance swimming equivalent to mountaineering's Seven Summits. She used swimming to push through the adversity of her injury.

"I don't see myself as crazy," she said. "I'm just Kim and I like to swim."[67]

Two recent academic papers provided a useful insight into how some athletes can turn adversity to their advantage. The first was a paper published in *Psychology of Sport and Exercise*[68], which looked at adversity and how it impacted growth-related experiences of several elite competitive swimmers. The findings provided support for the association between adversity and growth. Autobiographies of Olympic swimming champions were sampled covering four countries and seven Olympic Games.

Michael Phelps, hailed as the world's most successful and decorated Olympian - he has won twenty-eight Olympic medals - struggled with ADHD in grade school, as well as having his father leave home when Phelps was seven.

Mark Tewksbury of Canada, gold medalist in the 1988 Seoul games, recalled how homophobic graffiti on his school locker "sent me on a path that brought me to the height of Olympic sport."

Ryk Neethling of South Africa, gold medalist in the 1996 Atlanta games, described a serious shoulder injury "as if I had been sentenced to death," and his childhood stutter as "the most traumatic thing."

Amanda Beard, of the United States, double-gold medalist in the 1996 Atlanta games, characterized her childhood dyslexia and obsessive-compulsive behavior as years of adolescent difficulty and mortification.

Ian Thorpe of Australia, a five-times old medalist in the 2000 Sydney games, recounted how he spent a lot of his life "battling what I can only describe as crippling depression."

67  www.theguardian.com/sport/2017/oct/20/lim-chambers
68  *Psychology of Sport and Exercise* "Sink or swim: Adversity – and growth-related experiences in Olympic swimming champions." Howells & Fletcher: 2015; 16: 37-48

The study's authors evaluations concluded that the swimmers studied in their research ultimately thrived in the face of adversity by adopting strategies that helped them to overcome their experiences and to flourish not just as athletes, but as people. It is interesting that the athletes seemed to develop because of their adversity, not just despite it.

The second was a paper published in the *Journal of Science and Medicine in Sport*[69] described how experiencing some adversity can have beneficial outcomes for growth and development. The study interviewed ten Olympic gold medalists from several different sports. The findings indicated that adversity-related experiences were considered essential by the athletes to reach their peak performances. Adverse experiences included repeated sporting failure (e.g. not being selected), the death of a family member, and dealing with serious injury. The study concludes that adversity-related experiences offered potential development opportunities if they were "carefully and purposefully harnessed."

I have found a saying attributed to Henry Ford relevant and motivational. "There are people who say they can't and there are people who say they can. In both cases, they are usually right," goes the saying.

George Monbiot, a journalist with *The Guardian* newspaper, wrote about his reaction to a prostate cancer diagnosis. He was tempted to wallow in "why me?" self-pity but quickly reminded himself that he needed to focus on how much worse it could be. He especially railed against his condition being "scored." With prostate cancer, a one-to-ten ranking is used, based on the severity of progression. He decided to invent his own scale, which he called the "Shitstorm Scale."

He measured how his condition compared to other adversities, such as more severe health problems or family tragedies. He used the scale to remind himself that his bad luck was in fact a reminder of how lucky he was. With the love and

<hr>

69  *Journal of Science and Medicine in Sport* "What doesn't kill me: Adversity-related experiences are vital in the development of superior Olympic performance." Sarkar M et al. 2014; 18: 475-479

support of his family and friends, he concluded that his Shitstorm Scale score was a mere two out of ten.

Taking everything from Olympic athletes to heroic swimmers to post-lung transplant experiences into account, I have devised my own list of considerations and actions when faced with adversity. Here it is for consideration:

1. Accept that adversity occurs and that you can get through it. Identify what will help you get through the adversity, and do that thing (note: it may not necessarily be swimming);
2. Differentiate between events you can control and those you cannot. Focus on the former, not the latter;
3. Accept and be thankful for the support of your family and friends;
4. Be grateful for what you do have, not disappointed by what you do not have;
5. Set a goal. Put a photo of your goal in a visible place (e.g. fridge, desk, mirror) so you can see it several times every day;
6. Physically exercise to the highest level that is accessible to you (after checking with your doctor, of course), even if it is only walking. If possible, include, aerobic, resistance training and flexibility training. When you feel tired, just keep going;
7. Remind yourself that what doesn't kill you makes your stronger;
8. Be positive and upbeat, even if you don't feel like it;
9. Don't make excuses;
10. In a medical scenario, take all medication as prescribed by your doctor as if your life depends upon it;
11. Register as an organ, eye and tissue donor (and tell everyone about your decision);
12. Go back to the top of this list and read it again.

My goal is to demonstrate that living life to the fullest is possible in adverse conditions, and that you can get through adversity if you frame it the right way.

Swimming through adversity is one approach. Other approaches may be running, cycling, walking, singing, dancing, laughing, meditating, or even breathing through adversity. Whatever your approach, there is often a way through the most difficult challenges in life. You just have to find it.

# CHAPTER FIFTEEN: COOL-DOWN

*The longest surviving single lung-transplant patient is Veronica Dwyer (Ireland, b. 22 March 1941) who has lived 29 years and 129 days since her transplant on 19 May 1988 in Harefield, Middlesex, UK, as verified on 25 September 2017[70].*

- Guinness World Records

### Ten years post-transplant

I sat down with Julie, Zander and Riley a few weeks before the tenth anniversary of my double-lung transplant. Any ordeal like a family member's illness impacts everyone. I believe it is often harder on everyone else than it is on the person who is actually ill. I was interested in what they remembered and understood about the transplant. Zander was now eighteen, Riley sixteen. Ten years before, they were children of eight and six.

"I remember waking up one morning in the hotel," Riley said. "You and Mom were gone. I remember being nervous and excited. It was one of the dry runs."

"I remember popcorn and pancakes at the hotel!" Zander volunteered. Riley rolled her eyes.

"I really didn't understand that it was life or death," said Riley. "I didn't get that. We knew you were there to get better and that you were skinny. I thought you were there to get fatter!"

"I think I did understand what was at stake," said Zander, pensively. "Based on what Mom had told me and with my limited interaction with people at the hospital, I got the sense that the doctors were smart and knew what they were doing."

"When they described that they were going to take someone's lungs and put them in Dad, I accepted the explanation. I wasn't nervous or upset. I knew it would work out. I felt excited that you were going to get better," he said.

---

70  www.guinessworldrecords.com. Accessed 3/14/2018

"Were you scared?" I asked.

"No," said Riley. "Someone bought us kites, and I remember flying them outside. It was really windy. Mine got stuck in a tree."

I asked them about their experience at school around that time and how their teachers reacted. Both children stayed in elementary school in Denver for most of the time but came to visit us for a few two-week blocks.

"I remember repeating that my Dad was getting a double-lung transplant without really understanding what that meant," said Riley.

"One of my teachers said how odd it was that we were so calm," said Zander. "She kept saying "it'll all be okay" and "not to worry." I told her that I wasn't worried!"

Julie laughed. She was relieved that both children remembered meals and playing and had not been uneasy or panicked. The fact that they assumed that everything was going to work out told her something important.

"It tells me that I did my job. We kept you included but not immersed," she said. "There was so much stress, so much uncertainty. The fact that you both had such certainty was really great for me," said Julie. She had tears in her eyes.

"The fact that you stayed in a place of knowing helped me get through the adversity a million different times," she said.

She paused. "Just as long as I don't have to swim."

---

# ACKNOWLEDGEMENTS

Thank you to the following people for their amazing contribution and support:

Julie Busboom, Zander Maitland and Riley Maitland; Scott Palmer, MD, and the pre- and post-lung transplant team at Duke University Medical Center; May Maitland; John and Lori Maitland; Dorothy Maitland and Ailsa Robertson; Bill and Bette Maitland; William Maitland; Margo Willox and Kathleen Paton; Larry and Henna Busboom; Marc Bozon; Wanda and Aysha Hellevang; Jean Cornec; the Wham Boys (in alphabetical order to avoid arguments): Struan Douglas, Stephen Leonard, Jonathan O'Hara, Neville Prentice, James Richardson, Stephen Robertson, Andrew Stephen.

And thank you for kindly sharing your stories and expertise:

Raffaella Bruno-Pinto, Scott Coe, Kenneth Douglas, Leslie Durant, Steve Farber, Jeff Goldstein, Anastasia Henry, Scott Johnson, Chris Klug, Marika Page, Kimi Tasker, James Watson, Lisa Wickerson, and Emma Willox.

And a special thank you, with gratitude and respect, to the Burton family: Eddie, Pam, Noah, and Hunter.

# RESOURCES

Organizations making a real difference to lung health and organ donation awareness are set out below, along with links on how to donate to them:

Duke University Medical Center
Duke Health Development
710 W. Main Street, Suite 200
Durham, NC 27701
To make a donation, please go to:
www.gifts.duke.edu/dukehealth
Select: Palmer Lung Transplant Research Fund

Lung Transplant Foundation
*Breathing Life into Lung Transplant Research*
1249 Kildare Farm Road, Suite 323
Cary, NC 27511
https://lungtransplantfoundation.org
To make a donation, please go to:
https://lungtransplantfoundation.org/donate/

American Transplant Foundation
*Connecting People to Life*®
600 17th Street, Suite 2515 South
Denver, CO 80202
To make a donation, please go to:
https://atf.donordrive.col

Chris Klug Foundation
110 E Hallam st#102b,
ASPEN, 81611-1876
PO Box#64 Aspen, CO 81612

To make a donation, please go to:
https://chrisklugfoundation.org/
ourorgandonationprograms

To register as an organ donor, or to learn more, please go to:
Australia: www.donatelife.gov.au
Canada: www.organ-donation-works.org
France: www.dondorganes.fr
Germany: www.dso.de
Italy: www.trapianti.salute.gov.it
Ireland: www.organdonation.ie
Mexico: www.gob.mx/cenatra
Netherlands: www.donorregister.nl
New Zealand: www.donor.co.nz
Russia: www.transpl.ru
Spain: www.ont.es
South Africa: www.odf.org.za
United Kingdom: www.organdonation.nhs.uk
United States: www.organdonor.gov

or search online "how to be an organ donor" in your
country.

Updated information on the author:
www.gavinswims.life

CPSIA information can be obtained
at www.ICGtesting.com
Printed in the USA
FSHW02n1857300618
50013FS